Keto Diet Cookbook For Beginners

300 Mouthwatering, Hidh-Protein, and Low-Carb Recipes to Live Healthy Life. This is a Resource Anyone Who Wants to Start Their Ketogenic Journey and Improve Well-Being

The ketogenic (keto) diet is a high-fat, low-carbohydrate eating plan designed to shift the body's metabolism from burning glucose (derived from carbohydrates) to burning ketones (derived from fats). This metabolic state is known as ketosis.

Key components of the keto diet include:

1. **Macronutrient Ratio**: Typically, the diet comprises about 70-75% fats, 20-25% protein, and only about 5-10% carbohydrates.
2. **Food Choices**: It emphasizes foods like meat, fish, eggs, dairy, nuts, seeds, and low-carb vegetables while limiting grains, sugars, fruits, and starchy vegetables.

Benefits of the Keto Diet:

1. **Weight Loss**: Many people experience rapid weight loss due to reduced carbohydrate intake, leading to decreased insulin levels and fat burning.
2. **Improved Blood Sugar Control**: The diet can help stabilize blood sugar levels, making it beneficial for those with type 2 diabetes.
3. **Increased Energy and Focus**: Once adapted, individuals often report improved energy levels and mental clarity due to the steady supply of energy from fats.
4. **Reduced Hunger and Cravings**: High fat and protein intake can lead to increased satiety, reducing the likelihood of overeating.
5. **Potential Health Benefits**: Some studies suggest that the keto diet may have positive effects on certain neurological disorders, such as epilepsy, and may also aid in reducing inflammation.

However, it's essential to approach the keto diet with careful planning and possibly under medical supervision, especially for those with preexisting health conditions.

Table of contents

Crispy Chicken Drumsticks

INGREDIENTS
- · 8 chicken drumsticks,
- · 6 slices bacon, cooked and crumbled
- · 3/4 cup Greek yogurt
- · 3oz shredded coconut, unsweetened
- · 1/2 cup olive oil
- · 1 tsp smoked paprika Garlic powder, optional
- · Salt and pepper Low Carb Coleslaw
- · 4 cups shredded cabbage
- · 1/2 cup mayonnaise, low-carb
- · 2 tbsp apple cider vinegar
- · 1 tbsp powdered erythritol salt and pepper to taste

DIRECTIONS
1. Place drumsticks to a large bowl and add Greek yogurt, smoked paprika, salt, pepper, and a pinch of garlic powder.
2. With clean hands, coat each drumstick with the marinade and refrigerate for 30 minutes.
3. Meanwhile, add coconut, bacon, and salt and pepper to a food processor.
4. Pulse a couple of times and set aside.

No Bake Chocolate Cake

INGREDIENTS
- · 1 1/2 cup heavy cream
- · 7 oz dark chocolate, sugar-free
- · 1/2 cup butter
- · 1/4 cup erythritol
- · 1 tsp salt
- · 1/2 cup pumpkin seeds
- · 1/4 cup pecans, chopped

DIRECTIONS
1. In a nonstick pan, whisk together heavy cream and erythritol.
2. Bring to a boil over medium-low heat and gently simmer for 2 minutes.
3. Add chopped chocolate and butter.
4. Stir well until chocolate has completely melted.
5. Stir in pumpkin seeds and pecans.
6. Sprinkle salt.
7. Transfer chocolate mixture into a dish and place in the fridge over night.
8. Enjoy and Happy New Year.

Smoked Salmon and Asparagus Frittata

INGREDIENTS
- · 9 eggs
- · 3.5 oz smoked salmon, sliced
- · 5 oz asparagus, chopped
- · 3.5 oz mozzarella cheese, shredded
- · 3.5 oz parmesan cheesed, shredded
- · 1 cup heavy cream
- · 1/4 cup green onion, chopped
- · salt and pepper, butter-optional for serving

DIRECTIONS
1. Preheat oven to 350F and line a round 8 inch baking pan with parchment paper.
2. Whisk eggs in a large bowl and add heavy cream, mozzarella, parmesan, salt and pepper.
3. Mix in chopped asparagus and sliced salmon.
4. Fold in green onions.
5. Mix until combined.
6. Pour egg mixture into prepared pan.
7. Bake in the oven for 35-40 minutes or until eggs are set and golden brown at the top.
8. Serve with butter.

Avocado Hummus

INGREDIENTS
- 3 avocados
- 2 garlic cloves, minced
- 1/2 lemon, juice
- 1/4 cup tahini butter
- 1/4 cup parsley, fresh
- 1/4 cup olive oil
- 1 tsp cumin, ground
- 1/2 tsp salt
- crushed red pepper flakes to taste
- sliced cucumbers

DIRECTIONS
1. Add all ingredients to a food processor and blend until completely smooth.
2. Transfer to a serving bowl and sprinkle crushed red pepper flakes.
3. Serve with sliced cucumber.

Bran Muffins

INGREDIENTS
- 2 large eggs, slightly beaten
- 1 cup/240 ml buttermilk or plain yogurt
- ½ cup/120 ml barely melted unsalted butter
- ½ cup/ 60 ml maple syrup
- ½ cup /.75 oz. /20 g unprocessed wheat bran or oat bran
- ½ cup/ 4 oz. / 115 g plain, unsweetened bran cereal
- 1 cup/ 4 oz. / 115 g whole wheat pastry flour
- ¼ cup/ 1.25 oz. /35 g natural cane sugar
- 1 tsp baking soda
- 1 tsp aluminum-free baking powder
- 1 tsp fine-grain sea salt

DIRECTIONS
Preheat the oven to 400 F/205 C with a rack in the middle of the oven.
Generously butter a standard 12-cup muffin
pan.
In a large bowl, whisk together the eggs, buttermilk, melted butter, and maple syrup.
Sprinkle the bran cereal across
the top, stir, and allow the mixture to sit for 5 minutes.
In the meantime, in a separate small bowl, whisk together the flour, sugar, baking soda, baking powder, and salt.

Sprinkle the dry ingredients over the top of the wet and stir until just combined.
Immediately fill each muffin cup
three-quarters full.
Bake for 18-22 minutes, until the edges of the muffins begin to brown and the tops have set.
Let cool for 5 minutes
in the pan, then turn the muffins out of the pan to cool completely on a wire rack.

Keto Avocado Egg Salad

INGREDIENTS
- · - 2 ripe avocados
- · - 4 hard-boiled eggs
- · - 1 tablespoon mayonnaise
- · - 1 tablespoon mustard
- · - Salt and pepper to taste
- · - Chopped chives or green onions

DIRECTIONS
1. In a bowl, mash the avocados.
2. Chop the hard-boiled eggs and add them to the avocado.
3. Stir in mayonnaise, mustard, salt, and pepper.
4. Mix well and garnish with chives or green onions if desired.

Cauliflower Fried Rice

INGREDIENTS
- · - 1 small head of cauliflower, riced
- · - 2 tablespoons olive oil
- · - 2 eggs, beaten
- · - 1 cup mixed vegetables (like bell peppers, peas, and carrots)
- · - 2 tablespoons soy sauce (or coconut aminos for a lower-carb option)
- · - Green onions for garnish

DIRECTIONS
. Heat olive oil in a pan over medium heat.
2. Add the riced cauliflower and mixed vegetables; cook until tender.
3. Push the mixture to one side of the pan, add beaten eggs to the other side, and scramble them.
4. Once the eggs are cooked, mix everything together and add soy sauce.
5. Garnish with green onions before serving.

Zucchini Noodles with Pesto

INGREDIENTS
- · - 2 medium zucchinis, spiralized
- · - 1/2 cup basil pesto (store-bought or homemade)
- · - 1 tablespoon olive oil
- · - Salt and pepper to taste
- · - Grated Parmesan cheese

DIRECTIONS
1. In a skillet, heat olive oil over medium heat.
2. Add zucchini noodles and sauté for 2-3 minutes until just tender.
3. Remove from heat, stir in pesto, and season with salt and pepper.
4. Top with grated Parmesan cheese if desired.

Keto Chicken Alfredo

INGREDIENTS

- ·   - 2 chicken breasts, cooked and sliced
- ·   - 1 cup heavy cream
- ·   - 1/2 cup grated Parmesan cheese
- ·   - 2 tablespoons butter
- ·   - 2 cloves garlic, minced
- ·   - Salt and pepper to taste
- ·   - Fresh parsley for garnish

DIRECTIONS

. In a skillet, melt butter over medium heat and sauté garlic until fragrant.

2. Add heavy cream and bring to a simmer.

3. Stir in Parmesan cheese, and season with salt and pepper.

4. Add sliced chicken to the sauce and cook until heated through.

5. Garnish with fresh parsley before serving.

Keto Chocolate Mug Cake

INGREDIENTS

- ·   - 4 tablespoons almond flour
- ·   - 2 tablespoons cocoa powder
- ·   - 1 tablespoon erythritol (or preferred sweetener)
- ·   - 1/8 teaspoon baking powder
- ·   - 1 egg
- ·   - 3 tablespoons almond milk
- ·   - 1 tablespoon melted butter
- ·   - A few drops of vanilla extract

DIRECTIONS

1. In a microwave-safe mug, mix almond flour, cocoa powder, erythritol, and baking powder.

2. Add the egg, almond milk, melted butter, and vanilla; mix until smooth.

3. Microwave on high for about 60-90 seconds, or until cooked through.

4. Allow to cool slightly before enjoying.

Keto Cobb Salad

INGREDIENTS

- ·   - 4 cups mixed greens (romaine, spinach, etc.)
- ·   - 1 cup cooked chicken breast, diced
- ·   - 1/2 avocado, sliced
- ·   - 2 hard-boiled eggs, chopped
- ·   - 1/2 cup cherry tomatoes, halved
- ·   - 1/4 cup blue cheese, crumbled
- ·   - 4 strips of crispy bacon, crumbled
- ·   - Olive oil and vinegar for dressing
- ·   - Salt and pepper to taste

DIRECTIONS

1. In a large bowl, layer the mixed greens.

2. Arrange the chicken, avocado, eggs, tomatoes, blue cheese, and bacon on top.

3. Drizzle with olive oil and vinegar, and season with salt and pepper before serving.

Caesar Salad with Grilled Shrimp

INGREDIENTS

- · - 4 cups romaine lettuce, chopped
- · - 1 pound shrimp, peeled and deveined
- · - 2 tablespoons olive oil
- · - 1 teaspoon garlic powder
- · - Salt and pepper to taste
- · - 1/4 cup Parmesan cheese, grated
- · - Caesar dressing

DIRECTIONS

. In a bowl, toss shrimp with olive oil, garlic powder, salt, and pepper.

2. Grill shrimp until cooked through, about 2-3 minutes per side.

3. In a large bowl, combine romaine lettuce, grilled shrimp, Parmesan cheese, and Caesar dressing. Toss to combine.

Mediterranean Salad

INGREDIENTS

- · - 2 cups chopped cucumbers
- · - 1 cup cherry tomatoes, halved
- · - 1/2 cup red onion, thinly sliced
- · - 1/2 cup Kalamata olives, pitted and halved
- · - 1/2 cup feta cheese, crumbled
- · - 2 tablespoons olive oil
- · - 1 tablespoon red wine vinegar
- · - 1 teaspoon dried oregano
- · - Salt and pepper to taste

DIRECTIONS

. In a large bowl, combine cucumbers, cherry tomatoes, red onion, olives, and feta cheese.

2. In a small bowl, whisk together olive oil, red wine vinegar, oregano, salt, and pepper.

3. Drizzle the dressing over the salad and toss gently to combine.

Avocado Chicken Salad

INGREDIENTS

- · - 2 cups cooked chicken, shredded
- · - 1 ripe avocado, mashed
- · - 1/4 cup mayonnaise
- · - 1 tablespoon lime juice
- · - 1/4 cup celery, diced
- · - Salt and pepper to taste
- · - Lettuce leaves for serving

DIRECTIONS

1. In a bowl, combine shredded chicken, mashed avocado, mayonnaise, lime juice, celery, salt, and pepper.

2. Mix well until combined.

3. Serve on lettuce leaves for a refreshing meal.

Broccoli Salad

INGREDIENTS

- · - 2 cups broccoli florets, blanched
- · - 1/2 cup cooked bacon, crumbled
- · - 1/4 cup red onion, finely chopped
- · - 1/4 cup sunflower seeds
- · - 1/4 cup mayonnaise
- · - 1 tablespoon apple cider vinegar
- · - Salt and pepper to taste

DIRECTIONS

1. In a large bowl, combine blanched broccoli, bacon, red onion, and sunflower seeds.

2. In a separate bowl, whisk together mayonnaise, apple cider vinegar, salt, and pepper.

3. Pour the dressing over the salad and toss to combine.

Keto Beef Stroganoff

INGREDIENTS

- · - 1 pound beef sirloin, thinly sliced
- · - 2 tablespoons olive oil
- · - 1 cup mushrooms, sliced
- · - 2 cloves garlic, minced
- · - 1 cup beef broth
- · - 1 cup heavy cream
- · - 2 tablespoons Dijon mustard
- · - Salt and pepper to taste
- · - Fresh parsley for garnish

DIRECTIONS

1. Heat olive oil in a skillet over medium heat. Add beef and cook until browned. Remove and set aside.

2. In the same skillet, add mushrooms and garlic, sauté until mushrooms are tender.

3. Pour in beef broth, heavy cream, and Dijon mustard. Stir to combine and simmer for a few minutes.

4. Return the beef to the skillet, season with salt and pepper, and cook until heated through. Garnish with parsley before serving.

Keto Chicken Parmesan

INGREDIENTS

- · - 2 chicken breasts, pounded thin
- · - 1 cup almond flour
- · - 1/2 cup grated Parmesan cheese
- · - 1 egg, beaten
- · - 1 cup marinara sauce (sugar-free)
- · - 1 cup shredded mozzarella cheese
- · - Olive oil for frying

DIRECTIONS

1. Preheat the oven to 400°F (200°C).

2. In a bowl, mix almond flour and Parmesan cheese. Dip chicken breasts into the egg, then coat with the almond flour mixture.

3. Heat olive oil in a skillet over medium heat. Fry the chicken until golden on both sides.

4. Place the chicken in a baking dish, top with marinara sauce and mozzarella cheese. Bake for 15-20 minutes until the cheese is bubbly.

Keto Pork Chops with Creamy Garlic Sauce

INGREDIENTS

- ·   - 4 pork chops
- ·   - Salt and pepper to taste
- ·   - 2 tablespoons olive oil
- ·   - 3 cloves garlic, minced
- ·   - 1 cup heavy cream
- ·   - 1/2 cup chicken broth
- ·   - 1 teaspoon Italian seasoning
- ·   - Fresh parsley for garnish

DIRECTIONS

1. Season pork chops with salt and pepper. Heat olive oil in a skillet over medium-high heat and sear the chops until cooked through. Remove and set aside.

2. In the same skillet, add garlic and sauté for about 30 seconds. Then add heavy cream, chicken broth, and Italian seasoning. Simmer until thickened.

3. Return the pork chops to the skillet, coat with the sauce, and garnish with parsley before serving

Keto Meatballs

INGREDIENTS

- ·   - 1 pound ground beef or turkey
- ·   - 1/2 cup almond flour
- ·   - 1/4 cup grated Parmesan cheese
- ·   - 1 egg
- ·   - 2 cloves garlic, minced
- ·   - 1 teaspoon Italian seasoning
- ·   - Salt and pepper to taste
- ·   - Marinara sauce (sugar-free) for serving

DIRECTIONS

1. Preheat the oven to 400°F (200°C).

2. In a large bowl, combine ground meat, almond flour, Parmesan, egg, garlic, Italian seasoning, salt, and pepper. Mix well.

3. Form into meatballs and place on a baking sheet.

4. Bake for 20-25 minutes until cooked through. Serve with marinara sauce.

Keto Lemon Herb Grilled Chicken

INGREDIENTS

- ·   - 4 chicken thighs or breasts
- ·   - 1/4 cup olive oil
- ·   - Juice of 1 lemon
- ·   - 2 cloves garlic, minced
- ·   - 1 teaspoon dried oregano
- ·   - Salt and pepper to taste

DIRECTIONS

1. In a bowl, mix olive oil, lemon juice, garlic, oregano, salt, and pepper.

2. Add chicken to the marinade and let it sit for at least 30 minutes (or overnight in the fridge).

3. Preheat the grill to medium-high heat and grill the chicken for 6-7 minutes on each side until fully cooked.

Keto Chocolate Mousse

INGREDIENTS
- · - 1 cup heavy cream
- · - 2 tablespoons unsweetened cocoa powder
- · - 2 tablespoons erythritol (or preferred sweetener)
- · - 1 teaspoon vanilla extract
- · - A pinch of salt

DIRECTIONS
1. In a mixing bowl, whip the heavy cream until soft peaks form.
2. In a separate bowl, mix cocoa powder, erythritol, vanilla extract, and salt.
3. Gently fold the cocoa mixture into the whipped cream until well combined.
4. Spoon into serving dishes and refrigerate for at least 30 minutes before serving.

Keto Cheesecake Bite

INGREDIENTS
- · - 8 oz cream cheese, softened
- · - 1/2 cup erythritol
- · - 1 teaspoon vanilla extract
- · - 1 egg
- · - 1/2 teaspoon lemon juice

DIRECTIONS
1. Preheat the oven to 325°F (160°C) and line a mini muffin tin with paper liners.
2. In a mixing bowl, beat together cream cheese, erythritol, vanilla extract, egg, and lemon juice until smooth.
3. Pour the mixture into the prepared muffin tin and bake for 20-25 minutes until set.
4. Allow to cool and refrigerate before serving.

Keto Peanut Butter Cookies

INGREDIENTS
- · - 1 cup natural peanut butter (sugar-free)
- · - 1/2 cup erythritol
- · - 1 egg
- · - 1 teaspoon vanilla extract
- · - A pinch of salt

DIRECTIONS
1. Preheat the oven to 350°F (175°C) and line a baking sheet with parchment paper.
2. In a bowl, mix peanut butter, erythritol, egg, vanilla extract, and salt until well combined.
3. Scoop tablespoon-sized balls of dough onto the baking sheet and flatten slightly with a fork.
4. Bake for 10-12 minutes or until golden. Let cool before serving.

Keto Coconut Macaroons

INGREDIENTS
- · - 2 cups unsweetened shredded coconut
- · - 1/2 cup erythritol
- · - 2 egg whites
- · - 1 teaspoon vanilla extract
- · - A pinch of salt

DIRECTIONS

1. Preheat the oven to 325°F (160°C) and line a baking sheet with parchment paper.

2. In a bowl, mix shredded coconut, erythritol, egg whites, vanilla extract, and salt until combined.

3. Drop spoonfuls of the mixture onto the baking sheet.

4. Bake for 15-20 minutes until golden brown. Allow to cool before serving.

Keto Chocolate Chip Cookies

INGREDIENTS

- · - 2 cups almond flour
- · - 1/2 cup erythritol
- · - 1/2 teaspoon baking soda
- · - 1/4 teaspoon salt
- · - 1/2 cup unsalted butter, softened
- · - 1 teaspoon vanilla extract
- · - 1 large egg
- · - 1/2 cup sugar-free chocolate chips

DIRECTIONS

1. Preheat the oven to 350°F (175°C) and line a baking sheet with parchment paper.

2. In a bowl, cream together softened butter and erythritol.

3. Add egg and vanilla extract, mixing well.

4. In another bowl, combine almond flour, baking soda, and salt. Gradually add to the wet ingredients.

5. Fold in sugar-free chocolate chips.

6. Scoop dough onto the baking sheet and bake for 10-12 minutes or until golden.

Keto Almond Flour Bread

INGREDIENTS

- · - 2 cups almond flour
- · - 1/4 cup coconut flour
- · - 1/4 cup erythritol (or preferred sweetener)
- · - 1 tablespoon baking powder
- · - 1/2 teaspoon salt
- · - 4 large eggs
- · - 1/2 cup unsweetened almond milk
- · - 1/4 cup melted butter or coconut oil, - 1 teaspoon vanilla extract

DIRECTIONS

1. Preheat the oven to 350°F (175°C) and grease a loaf pan.

2. In a bowl, mix almond flour, coconut flour, erythritol, baking powder, and salt.

3. In another bowl, whisk together eggs, almond milk, melted butter, and vanilla extract.

4. Combine the wet and dry ingredients until well mixed.

5. Pour the batter into the prepared loaf pan and bake for 30-35 minutes until golden and a toothpick comes out clean.

Keto Chocolate Cake

INGREDIENTS

- · - 1 1/2 cups almond flour
- · - 1/2 cup unsweetened cocoa powder
- · - 1 cup erythritol
- · - 1 teaspoon baking powder

- · - 1/2 teaspoon baking soda
- · - 1/4 teaspoon salt
- · - 1/2 cup unsweetened almond milk
- · - 1/4 cup melted coconut oil
- · - 3 large eggs
- · - 1 teaspoon vanilla extract

DIRECTIONS

1. Preheat the oven to 350°F (175°C) and grease a round cake pan.
2. In a bowl, mix almond flour, cocoa powder, erythritol, baking powder, baking soda, and salt.
3. In another bowl, whisk together almond milk, melted coconut oil, eggs, and vanilla extract.
4. Combine the wet and dry ingredients until smooth.
5. Pour the batter into the prepared cake pan and bake for 25-30 minutes. Let cool before serving.

Keto Pumpkin Muffins

INGREDIENTS

- · - 1 cup almond flour
- · - 1/2 cup pumpkin puree (unsweetened)
- · - 1/4 cup erythritol
- · - 1/4 cup coconut flour
- · - 3 large eggs
- · - 1 teaspoon baking powder
- · - 1 teaspoon pumpkin spice
- · - 1/2 teaspoon vanilla extract
- · - A pinch of salt

DIRECTIONS

1. Preheat the oven to 350°F (175°C) and line a muffin tin with liners.
2. In a bowl, mix almond flour, coconut flour, erythritol, baking powder, pumpkin spice, and salt.
3. In another bowl, whisk together pumpkin puree, eggs, and vanilla extract.
4. Combine the wet and dry ingredients and mix until smooth.
5. Divide the batter into the muffin tin and bake for 20-25 minutes.

Keto Cheddar Biscuits

INGREDIENTS

- · - 2 cups almond flour
- · - 1 cup shredded cheddar cheese
- · - 2 large eggs
- · - 1/4 cup unsalted butter, melted
- · - 1 teaspoon baking powder
- · - 1/2 teaspoon garlic powder
- · - Salt and pepper to taste

DIRECTIONS

1. Preheat the oven to 375°F (190°C) and line a baking sheet with parchment paper.
2. In a bowl, combine almond flour, shredded cheddar cheese, baking powder, garlic powder, salt, and pepper.
3. In another bowl, mix eggs and melted butter.
4. Combine the wet and dry ingredients until a dough forms.
5. Drop spoonfuls of dough onto the baking sheet and bake for 15-20 minutes until golden.

Keto Snickerdoodle Cookies

INGREDIENTS

- · - 2 cups almond flour
- · - 1/2 cup erythritol
- · - 1/2 teaspoon baking powder
- · - 1 teaspoon cinnamon (plus extra for rolling)
- · - 1/4 teaspoon salt
- · - 1/2 cup unsalted butter, softened
- · - 1 large egg
- · - 1 teaspoon vanilla extract

DIRECTIONS

1. Preheat the oven to 350°F (175°C) and line a baking sheet with parchment paper.

2. In a bowl, mix almond flour, erythritol, baking powder, cinnamon, and salt.

3. In another bowl, cream together softened butter, egg, and vanilla extract.

4. Combine wet and dry ingredients to form a dough.

5. Roll dough into balls, then roll in a mixture of cinnamon and erythritol.

6. Place on the baking sheet and bake for 10-12 minutes.

Lemon Garlic Butter Fish

INGREDIENTS

- · - 4 fish fillets (such as cod, tilapia, or salmon)
- · - Salt and pepper (to taste)
- · - 2 tablespoons olive oil**
- · - 4 tablespoons unsalted butter**
- · - 4 cloves garlic (minced)
- · - 1 lemon (juiced and zested)
- · - 2 tablespoons fresh parsley (chopped, optional for garnish)
- · - Pinch of red pepper flakes (optional for heat)

DIRECTIONS

1. **Prepare the Fish**:

- Pat the fish fillets dry with paper towels. Season both sides with salt and pepper.

2. **Cook the Fish**:

- In a large skillet, heat the olive oil over medium-high heat. Add the fish fillets and cook for about 3-4 minutes on one side until golden brown.- Carefully flip the fillets and cook for another 3-4 minutes, or until the fish is cooked through and flakes easily with a fork. Remove the fish from the skillet and set aside.

3. **Make the Lemon Garlic Butter Sauce**:

- In the same skillet, reduce the heat to medium and add the butter. Once melted, add the minced garlic and sauté for about 1 minute until fragrant.- Stir in the lemon juice and lemon zest. If desired, add a pinch of red pepper flakes.

4. **Combine**:

- Return the cooked fish to the skillet, spooning the sauce over the fillets. Let it cook for an additional minute to heat through.

5. **Serve**: Transfer the fish to serving plates, drizzle with the sauce, and garnish with chopped parsley if desired. Serve immediately.

Crispy Parmesan Crusted Salmon

INGREDIENTS
- · - 4 salmon fillets (skin-on or skinless, about 6 ounces each)
- · - Salt and pepper (to taste)
- · - 1/2 cup grated Parmesan cheese
- · - 1/2 cup panko breadcrumbs
- · - 1 teaspoon garlic powder
- · - 1 teaspoon dried Italian herbs (such as oregano or basil)
- · - 2 tablespoons fresh parsley (chopped, optional for garnish)
- · - 3 tablespoons olive oil (divided)
- · - 1 tablespoon Dijon mustard (optional

DIRECTIONS

1. **Preheat the Oven**:
- Preheat your oven to 400°F (200°C).

2. **Prepare the Salmon**:
- Line a baking sheet with parchment paper or lightly grease it. Place the salmon fillets on the prepared baking sheet and season with salt and pepper.

3. **Make the Crust**:
- In a bowl, combine the grated Parmesan cheese, panko breadcrumbs, garlic powder, dried Italian herbs, and 1 tablespoon of olive oil. Mix until well combined.

4. **Coat the Salmon**:
- If using, spread a thin layer of Dijon mustard over the top of each salmon fillet. This will help the crust adhere better and add flavor.
- Press the Parmesan and breadcrumb mixture onto the top of each salmon fillet, ensuring an even coating.

5. **Drizzle with Olive Oil**:
- Drizzle the remaining 2 tablespoons of olive oil over the crusted salmon fillets.

6. **Bake the Salmon**:
- Place the baking sheet in the preheated oven and bake for about 12-15 minutes, or until the salmon is cooked through and the crust is golden and crispy. The internal temperature should reach 145°F (63°C).

7. **Serve**:
- Remove the salmon from the oven and let it rest for a couple of minutes. Garnish with fresh parsley if desired. Serve with your choice of sides, such as roasted vegetables or a salad.

Keto Garlic Butter Salmon

INGREDIENTS
- · - 4 salmon fillets
- · - 4 tablespoons butter
- · - 4 cloves garlic (minced)
- · - 1 tablespoon lemon juice
- · - Salt and pepper (to taste)
- · - Fresh parsley (chopped, for garnish)

DIRECTIONS

1. In a skillet, melt butter over medium heat. Add minced garlic and sauté for 1 minute until fragrant.
2. Season salmon fillets with salt and pepper. Place them in the skillet, skin-side down.
3. Cook for 5-6 minutes, then carefully flip and cook for another 3-4 minutes until cooked through.
4. Drizzle with lemon juice and garnish with parsley before serving.

Keto Lemon Dill Baked Salmon

INGREDIENTS
- · - 4 salmon fillets
- · - 2 tablespoons olive oil
- · - Juice of 1 lemon
- · - 2 teaspoons dried dill (or fresh dill)
- · - Salt and pepper (to taste)
- · - Lemon slices (for garnish)

DIRECTIONS
1. Preheat the oven to 375°F (190°C).
2. In a bowl, mix olive oil, lemon juice, dill, salt, and pepper. Place salmon fillets on a baking sheet and brush with the mixture.
3. Bake for 15-20 minutes or until cooked through.
4. Garnish with lemon slices and serve.

Keto Salmon with Creamy Spinach

INGREDIENTS
- · - 4 salmon fillets
- · - 2 tablespoons olive oil
- · - 2 cups fresh spinach
- · - 1/2 cup heavy cream
- · - 1/4 cup grated Parmesan cheese
- · - 1 clove garlic (minced)
- · - Salt and pepper (to taste)

DIRECTIONS
1. In a skillet, heat olive oil over medium heat. Add salmon fillets and cook for 4-5 minutes on each side until cooked through. Remove and set aside.
2. In the same skillet, add garlic and spinach, cooking until the spinach is wilted.
3. Stir in the heavy cream and Parmesan cheese, cooking until thickened. Season with salt and pepper.
4. Serve the salmon topped with the creamy spinach.

Keto Teriyaki Salmon Bowls

INGREDIENTS
- · 4 salmon fillets
- · - 1/4 cup soy sauce (or coconut aminos for a lower-carb option)
- · - 2 tablespoons sesame oil
- · - 1 tablespoon ginger (grated)
- · - 1 tablespoon garlic (minced)
- · - 1 tablespoon sesame seeds (for garnish)
- · - Green onions (sliced, for garnish)

DIRECTIONS
1. In a bowl, whisk together soy sauce, sesame oil, ginger, and garlic.
2. Marinate the salmon in the mixture for about 30 minutes.
3. Preheat the grill or skillet and cook the salmon for 4-5 minutes on each side until cooked through.
4. Serve garnished with sesame seeds and green onions.

Garlic Butter Shrimp

INGREDIENTS

- · - 1 pound large shrimp, peeled and deveined
- · - 4 tablespoons butter
- · - 4 cloves garlic, minced
- · - 1 teaspoon paprika
- · - Salt and pepper (to taste)
- · - 2 tablespoons fresh parsley, chopped (for garnish)
- · - Lemon wedges (for serving)

DIRECTIONS

1. In a large skillet, melt butter over medium heat. Add minced garlic and sauté for about 1 minute until fragrant.

2. Add shrimp to the skillet, seasoning with paprika, salt, and pepper. Cook for 2-3 minutes on each side until the shrimp are pink and opaque.

3. Remove from heat and garnish with fresh parsley. Serve with lemon wedges.

Keto Shrimp Tacos with Avocado Crema

INGREDIENTS

- · - 1 pound shrimp, peeled and deveined
- · - 1 tablespoon olive oil
- · - 1 teaspoon chili powder
- · - 1 teaspoon cumin
- · - Salt and pepper (to taste)
- · - Lettuce leaves (for wrapping)
- · - For the Avocado Crema:
- · - 1 ripe avocado
- · - 1/4 cup sour cream
- · - Juice of 1 lime,- Salt (to taste)

DIRECTIONS

1. In a bowl, mix shrimp with olive oil, chili powder, cumin, salt, and pepper.

2. Heat a skillet over medium heat and cook shrimp for 3-4 minutes until cooked through.

3. For the avocado crema, blend avocado, sour cream, lime juice, and salt until smooth.

4. Serve shrimp in lettuce leaves topped with avocado crema.

Creamy Cajun Shrimp

INGREDIENTS

- · - 1 pound shrimp, peeled and deveined
- · - 2 tablespoons olive oil
- · - 1 tablespoon Cajun seasoning
- · - 1 cup heavy cream
- · - 1/2 cup chicken broth
- · - 1/4 cup grated Parmesan cheese
- · - 2 tablespoons fresh parsley, chopped (for garnish)

DIRECTIONS

1. In a skillet, heat olive oil over medium heat. Add shrimp and Cajun seasoning; cook for 3-4 minutes until shrimp are pink.

2. Remove shrimp and set aside. In the same skillet, add chicken broth and heavy cream, bringing it to a simmer.

3. Stir in Parmesan cheese and return shrimp to the skillet. Cook for an additional 2-3 minutes until heated through.
4. Garnish with fresh parsley before serving.

Shrimp and Zucchini Noodles
INGREDIENTS
· -1 pound shrimp, peeled and deveined
· - 2 medium zucchinis (spiralized into noodles)
· - 2 tablespoons olive oil
· - 3 cloves garlic, minced
· - Salt and pepper (to taste)
· - 1/2 teaspoon red pepper flakes (optional)
· - Fresh basil or parsley (for garnish)
DIRECTIONS
1. In a large skillet, heat olive oil over medium heat. Add garlic and sauté for about 1 minute.
2. Add shrimp and cook for 3-4 minutes until pink. Season with salt, pepper, and red pepper flakes.
3. Add zucchini noodles to the skillet and toss everything together for another 1-2 minutes until the noodles are slightly tender.
4. Garnish with fresh basil or parsley before serving.

Keto Garlic Butter Shrimp
INGREDIENTS
· - 1 pound (450 g) large shrimp, peeled and deveined
· - 4 tablespoons (60 g) unsalted butter
· - 4 cloves garlic, minced
· - 1 teaspoon paprika
· - Salt and pepper, to taste
· - 2 tablespoons fresh parsley, chopped (for garnish)
· - Lemon wedges
DIRECTIONS
1. **Prep the Shrimp:** Start by rinsing the shrimp under cold water and patting them dry with paper towels. This helps them sear better.
2. **Melt the Butter:** In a large skillet, melt the butter over medium heat. Make sure it doesn't burn; you want it to be bubbly but not browned.
3. **Add Garlic:** Once the butter is melted, add the minced garlic to the skillet. Sauté for about 30 seconds until fragrant, being careful not to let it brown.
4. **Cook the Shrimp:** Add the shrimp to the skillet in a single layer. Season with paprika, salt, and pepper. Cook for about 2-3 minutes on one side until they turn pink, then flip and cook for an additional 1-2 minutes until fully cooked.
5. **Garnish and Serve:** Remove from heat, sprinkle with fresh parsley, and serve immediately with lemon wedges on the side.

Keto Creamy Tuscan Salmon

INGREDIENTS

- - 2 salmon fillets (about 6 oz each)
- - Salt and pepper, to taste
- - 2 tablespoons olive oil
- - 2 cups spinach, fresh
- - 1/2 cup heavy cream
- - 1/4 cup sun-dried tomatoes, chopped
- - 1/4 cup grated parmesan cheese
- - 2 cloves garlic, minced
- - 1 teaspoon Italian seasoning

DIRECTIONS

1. **Season the Salmon:** Pat the salmon fillets dry and season them with salt and pepper on both sides.
2. **Sear the Salmon:** In a large skillet, heat the olive oil over medium-high heat. Once hot, add the salmon fillets skin-side down. Cook for about 4-5 minutes until the skin is crispy, then flip and cook for another 3-4 minutes until cooked through. Remove the salmon from the skillet and set aside.
3. **Make the Creamy Sauce:** In the same skillet, lower the heat to medium and add minced garlic. Sauté for about 30 seconds until fragrant. Add the chopped sun-dried tomatoes and cook for 1-2 minutes.
4. **Add Spinach and Cream:** Stir in the spinach and cook until wilted. Pour in the heavy cream, then add the parmesan cheese and Italian seasoning. Mix well and let it simmer for a couple of minutes until the sauce thickens slightly.
5. **Combine and Serve:** Return the salmon to the skillet, spooning the sauce over it. Cook for another minute to heat through. Serve hot with additional spinach or a side salad.

Keto Parmesan-Crusted Chicken

INGREDIENTS

- - 4 boneless, skinless chicken breasts (about 6 oz each)
- - 1 cup grated Parmesan cheese
- - 1/2 cup almond flour
- - 2 teaspoons garlic powder
- - 1 teaspoon onion powder
- - 1 teaspoon Italian seasoning
- - Salt and pepper, to taste
- - 2 large eggs
- - 2 tablespoons olive oil
- - Fresh parsley, chopped (for garnish

DIRECTIONS

1. **Preheat the Oven:** Preheat your oven to 400°F (200°C). Line a baking sheet with parchment paper for easy cleanup.
2. **Prepare the Coating:** In a shallow bowl, combine the grated Parmesan cheese, almond flour, garlic powder, onion powder, Italian seasoning, salt, and pepper. Mix well to combine.
3. **Prepare the Eggs:** In another bowl, whisk the eggs until well beaten.
4. **Coat the Chicken:** Dip each chicken breast into the beaten eggs, allowing excess to drip off. Then, coat the chicken in the Parmesan mixture, pressing gently to ensure it adheres.
5. **Arrange on Baking Sheet:** Place the coated chicken breasts on the prepared baking sheet. Drizzle olive oil over the top of each piece to help with browning.
6. **Bake:** Bake in the preheated oven for about 25-30 minutes, or until the chicken is cooked through (internal temperature should reach 165°F or 74°C) and the coating is golden and crispy.

7. **Garnish and Serve:** Remove from the oven, garnish with fresh parsley, and serve hot with your choice of low-carb vegetables.

Keto Cheesy Broccoli Casserole

INGREDIENTS
- · - 4 cups fresh broccoli florets (about 1 large head)
- · - 1 cup shredded cheddar cheese
- · - 1 cup cream cheese, softened
- · - 1/2 cup sour cream
- · - 1/4 cup grated Parmesan cheese
- · - 1 teaspoon garlic powder
- · - 1 teaspoon onion powder
- · - Salt and pepper, to taste
- · - 1/2 cup cooked bacon bits (optional)
- · - 1/4 cup green onions, chopped (for garnish)

DIRECTIONS

1. **Preheat the Oven:** Preheat your oven to 350°F (175°C). Grease a 9x9-inch baking dish or similar size casserole dish.

2. **Blanch the Broccoli:** Bring a pot of salted water to a boil. Add the broccoli florets and blanch for about 2-3 minutes until bright green and slightly tender. Drain and rinse under cold water to stop the cooking process. Set aside.

3. **Prepare the Cheese Mixture:** In a large mixing bowl, combine the softened cream cheese, sour cream, garlic powder, onion powder, salt, and pepper. Mix until smooth and well combined.

4. **Combine Ingredients:** Add the blanched broccoli and half of the shredded cheddar cheese to the cream cheese mixture. If using, mix in the cooked bacon bits. Stir until everything is well coated.

5. **Transfer to Baking Dish:** Pour the broccoli mixture into the prepared baking dish. Spread it out evenly. Sprinkle the remaining shredded cheddar cheese and Parmesan cheese on top.

6. **Bake:** Bake in the preheated oven for 25-30 minutes, or until the cheese is bubbly and slightly golden.

7. **Garnish and Serve:** Remove from the oven and let cool for a few minutes. Garnish with chopped green onions before serving.

Keto Avocado & Bacon Egg Cups

INGREDIENTS
- · - 2 ripe avocados
- · - 4 large eggs
- · - 4 strips of cooked bacon, crumbled
- · - Salt and pepper, to taste
- · - Fresh chives or parsley, chopped (for garnish)

DIRECTIONS

1. **Preheat the Oven:** Preheat your oven to 425°F (220°C).

2. **Prepare the Avocados:** Cut the avocados in half and remove the pit. Scoop out a little extra flesh to make room for the egg.

3. **Place in a Baking Dish:** Place the avocado halves in a baking dish, ensuring they fit snugly to prevent tipping.

4. **Add Eggs:** Crack an egg into each avocado half. Sprinkle with salt, pepper, and crumbled bacon.

5. **Bake:** Bake in the preheated oven for about 12-15 minutes, or until the egg whites are set but the yolks are still runny.

6. **Garnish and Serve:** Remove from the oven, garnish with fresh chives or parsley, and serve immediately.

Keto Almond Flour Pancakes

INGREDIENTS

- · - 1 cup almond flour
- · - 2 large eggs
- · - 1/4 cup unsweetened almond milk (or any low-carb milk)
- · - 1 tablespoon erythritol (or your preferred sweetener)
- · - 1 teaspoon baking powder
- · - 1/2 teaspoon vanilla extract
- · - Butter or coconut oil (for cooking)

DIRECTIONS

1. **Mix Ingredients:** In a bowl, combine almond flour, erythritol, and baking powder. In another bowl, whisk together eggs, almond milk, and vanilla extract. Combine both mixtures and stir until smooth.
2. **Heat the Pan:** Heat a non-stick skillet over medium heat and add a little butter or coconut oil.
3. **Cook Pancakes:** Pour about 1/4 cup of batter onto the skillet for each pancake. Cook until bubbles form on the surface, about 2-3 minutes. Flip and cook for an additional 1-2 minutes until golden brown.
4. **Serve:** Serve warm with sugar-free syrup, fresh berries, or whipped cream.

Keto Chia Seed Pudding

INGREDIENTS

- · - 1/4 cup chia seeds
- · - 1 cup unsweetened almond milk (or any low-carb milk)
- · - 1 tablespoon erythritol or your preferred sweetener
- · - 1/2 teaspoon vanilla extract
- · - Fresh berries or nuts (for topping)

DIRECTIONS

1. **Combine Ingredients:** In a bowl or jar, mix chia seeds, almond milk, erythritol, and vanilla extract. Stir well to avoid clumping.
2. **Refrigerate:** Cover and refrigerate for at least 2 hours, or overnight, until the mixture thickens to a pudding-like consistency.
3. **Serve:** Stir well before serving and top with fresh berries or nuts.

Keto Egg Muffins

INGREDIENTS

- · 6 large eggs
- · - 1/2 cup bell peppers, diced
- · - 1/2 cup spinach, chopped
- · - 1/4 cup onion, diced
- · - 1/2 cup shredded cheese (cheddar or your choice)
- · - Salt and pepper, to taste
- · - Cooking spray or olive oil (for greasing the muffin tin)

DIRECTIONS

1. **Preheat the Oven:** Preheat your oven to 350°F (175°C) and grease a muffin tin with cooking spray or olive oil.

2. **Mix Ingredients:** In a bowl, whisk together the eggs, salt, and pepper. Stir in bell peppers, spinach, onion, and cheese.

3. **Fill Muffin Tin:** Pour the egg mixture evenly into the muffin cups, filling each about 2/3 full.

4. **Bake:** Bake for 18-20 minutes, or until the egg muffins are set and lightly golden on top.

5. **Cool and Serve:** Let cool slightly before removing from the muffin tin. Serve warm or store in the fridge for meal prep.

KetoChicken Salad Lettuce Wraps

INGREDIENTS

- · - 2 cups cooked chicken breast, shredded
- · - 1/2 cup mayonnaise
- · - 1/4 cup celery, chopped
- · - 1/4 cup red onion, finely chopped
- · - 1 tablespoon Dijon mustard
- · - Salt and pepper, to taste
- · - Lettuce leaves (romaine or butter lettuce)
- · - Optional: diced pickles or chopped walnuts for added crunch

DIRECTIONS

. **Mix Ingredients:** In a large bowl, combine the shredded chicken, mayonnaise, celery, red onion, Dijon mustard, salt, and pepper. Mix until well combined. If desired, add diced pickles or walnuts.

2. **Prepare Lettuce Wraps:** Wash and dry the lettuce leaves. Spoon the chicken salad mixture into the lettuce leaves.

3. **Serve:** Roll up the lettuce leaves and enjoy your wraps immediately, or store them in the fridge for a quick lunch option.

Keto Zucchini Noodles with Pesto and Shrimp

INGREDIENTS

- · - 2 medium zucchinis, spiralized into noodles
- · - 1 pound (450 g) shrimp, peeled and deveined
- · - 1/4 cup pesto (store-bought or homemade)
- · - 2 tablespoons olive oil
- · - 2 cloves garlic, minced
- · - Salt and pepper, to taste
- · - Grated Parmesan cheese (for garnish)

DIRECTIONS

1. **Sauté Shrimp:** In a large skillet, heat olive oil over medium heat. Add minced garlic and sauté for about 30 seconds until fragrant. Add shrimp, season with salt and pepper, and cook for about 3-4 minutes until pink and cooked through. Remove from the skillet and set aside.

2. **Cook Zoodles:** In the same skillet, add the spiralized zucchini noodles. Sauté for about 2-3 minutes until tender but still al dente.

3. **Combine and Serve:** Add the cooked shrimp back to the skillet and stir in the pesto until everything is well coated. Serve immediately with grated Parmesan cheese on top.

Keto Cauliflower Fried Rice

INGREDIENTS

- · - 1 medium head of cauliflower, grated or riced
- · - 2 tablespoons olive oil
- · - 2 large eggs, beaten
- · - 1 cup mixed vegetables (like bell peppers, peas, and carrots)
- · - 3 green onions, chopped
- · - 2 tablespoons soy sauce or coconut aminos
- · - Salt and pepper, to taste

DIRECTIONS

1. **Rice the Cauliflower:** Remove the leaves and stem from the cauliflower and grate it or pulse it in a food processor to create rice-sized pieces.

2. **Cook Vegetables:** In a large skillet or wok, heat olive oil over medium heat. Add the mixed vegetables and stir-fry for about 3-4 minutes until tender.

3. **Add Eggs:** Push the vegetables to one side of the skillet and pour the beaten eggs into the other side. Scramble the eggs until cooked through, then mix with the vegetables.

4. **Add Cauliflower Rice:** Stir in the cauliflower rice and soy sauce. Cook for an additional 5-7 minutes, stirring frequently, until the cauliflower is tender. Season with salt and pepper to taste.

5. **Garnish and Serve:** Top with chopped green onions and serve hot.

Keto Caprese Salad with Balsamic Glaze

INGREDIENTS

- · - 2 large tomatoes, sliced
- · - 8 oz (225 g) fresh mozzarella cheese, sliced
- · - Fresh basil leaves
- · - 3 tablespoons olive oil
- · - 2 tablespoons balsamic glaze
- · - Salt and pepper, to taste

DIRECTIONS

1. **Layer Ingredients:** On a serving platter, alternate layers of tomato slices, mozzarella slices, and basil leaves.

2. **Drizzle with Oil and Glaze:** Drizzle olive oil and balsamic glaze over the top. Season with salt and pepper to taste.

3. **Serve:** Serve immediately as a refreshing lunch or side dish.

Keto Beef and Broccoli Stir-Fry

NGREDIENTS

- · - 1 pound (450 g) beef flank steak, thinly sliced
- · - 2 cups broccoli florets
- · - 2 tablespoons soy sauce or coconut aminos
- · - 1 tablespoon sesame oil
- · - 2 tablespoons olive oil
- · - 2 cloves garlic, minced
- · - 1 tablespoon fresh ginger, minced
- · - Salt and pepper, to taste
- · - Sesame seeds (for garnish)

DIRECTIONS

1. **Marinate the Beef:** In a bowl, combine the sliced beef with soy sauce, sesame oil, garlic, ginger, salt, and pepper. Let it marinate for at least 15 minutes.

2. **Cook Broccoli:** In a large skillet, heat olive oil over medium heat. Add broccoli florets and stir-fry for about 3-4 minutes until tender. Remove from the skillet and set aside.
3. **Cook Beef:** In the same skillet, add the marinated beef in a single layer. Cook for about 2-3 minutes on each side until browned and cooked through.
4. **Combine and Serve:** Return the broccoli to the skillet, stir to combine, and heat through. Serve hot, garnished with sesame seeds.

Keto Creamy Tuscan Chicken

INGREDIENTS
- · - 4 boneless, skinless chicken thighs
- · - 1 tablespoon olive oil
- · - 3 cloves garlic, minced
- · - 1 cup heavy cream
- · - 1/2 cup sun-dried tomatoes, chopped
- · - 1 cup fresh spinach
- · - 1/4 cup grated Parmesan cheese
- · - Salt and pepper, to taste

DIRECTIONS
1. **Sear the Chicken:** In a large skillet, heat olive oil over medium-high heat. Season the chicken thighs with salt and pepper. Add them to the skillet and cook for about 5-6 minutes on each side until golden brown and cooked through. Remove and set aside.
2. **Make the Sauce:** In the same skillet, add minced garlic and sauté for about 30 seconds. Pour in the heavy cream, sun-dried tomatoes, spinach, and Parmesan cheese. Stir well and let it simmer for 3-5 minutes until the sauce thickens slightly.
3. **Combine and Serve:** Return the chicken to the skillet, spooning the sauce over it. Cook for an additional minute to heat through. Serve hot with a side of low-carb vegetables.

Keto Cauliflower Pizza

INGREDIENTS
- · - 1 medium head of cauliflower, grated or riced
- · - 1 cup shredded mozzarella cheese
- · - 1/4 cup grated Parmesan cheese
- · - 1 large egg
- · - 1 teaspoon Italian seasoning
- · - Salt and pepper, to taste
- · - Toppings of your choice (pepperoni, bell peppers, olives, etc.)
- · - Additional mozzarella cheese (for topping)

DIRECTIONS
1. **Preheat the Oven:** Preheat your oven to 450°F (230°C). Line a baking sheet with parchment paper.
2. **Prepare Cauliflower Crust:** In a large bowl, combine grated cauliflower, shredded mozzarella, Parmesan cheese, egg, Italian seasoning, salt, and pepper. Mix until well combined.
3. **Form the Crust:** Spread the mixture onto the prepared baking sheet, forming a round pizza shape about 1/4 inch thick.
4. **Bake the Crust:** Bake for 12-15 minutes until golden and crispy.
5. **Add Toppings:** Remove from the oven, add your desired toppings and extra mozzarella cheese, and return to the oven for another 5-7 minutes until the cheese is melted and bubbly.
6. **Slice and Serve:** Let cool slightly, slice, and serve.

Keto Stuffed Bell Peppers

INGREDIENTS
- · - 4 large bell peppers (any color)
- · - 1 pound (450 g) ground beef or turkey
- · - 1 cup cauliflower rice
- · - 1 can (14 oz) diced tomatoes, drained
- · - 1 teaspoon Italian seasoning
- · - Salt and pepper, to taste
- · - 1 cup shredded cheese (mozzarella or cheddar)
- · - Fresh parsley (for garnish)

DIRECTIONS

1.**Preheat the Oven:** Preheat your oven to 375°F (190°C). Cut the tops off the bell peppers and remove the seeds.

2. **Cook the Filling:** In a skillet, cook the ground beef over medium heat until browned. Stir in cauliflower rice, diced tomatoes, Italian seasoning, salt, and pepper. Cook for an additional 5-7 minutes until heated through.

3. **Stuff the Peppers:** Spoon the filling into each bell pepper, packing it down slightly. Place the stuffed peppers in a baking dish.

4. **Add Cheese:** Top each stuffed pepper with shredded cheese.

5. **Bake:** Cover the baking dish with foil and bake for 25 minutes. Remove the foil and bake for an additional 10-15 minutes until the cheese is melted and bubbly.

6. **Garnish and Serve:** Remove from the oven, garnish with fresh parsley, and serve.

Keto Chicken Crust Pizza

INGREDIENTS
- · - 2 cups cooked chicken, shredded (rotisserie chicken works well)
- · - 1 cup shredded mozzarella cheese,1 large egg
- · - 1/2 teaspoon garlic powder
- · - 1/2 teaspoon Italian seasoning
- · - Salt and pepper, to taste **Toppings:**
- · - 1/2 cup sugar-free pizza sauce
- · - 1 cup shredded mozzarella cheese (for topping)
- · - 1/4 cup grated Parmesan cheese
- · - Pepperoni slices,Sliced bell peppers
- · - Sliced olives

DIRECTIONS

1. **Preheat the Oven:** Preheat your oven to 400°F (200°C). Line a baking sheet with parchment paper.

2. **Prepare the Chicken Crust:** In a large bowl, combine the shredded chicken, 1 cup of shredded mozzarella cheese, egg, garlic powder, Italian seasoning, salt, and pepper. Mix well. Spread the mixture onto the prepared baking sheet, forming a round pizza shape about 1/2 inch thick.

3. **Bake the Crust:** Bake for 15-20 minutes until golden and firm.

4. **Add Toppings:** Spread sugar-free pizza sauce over the crust, sprinkle with remaining cheese and desired toppings.

5. **Final Bake:** Return to the oven for another 10-12 minutes until the cheese is melted and bubbly.

6. **Serve:** Let cool slightly before slicing and enjoy.

Keto Almond Flour Pizza

INGREDIENTS

- · - 2 cups almond flour, 1 large egg
- · - 1/4 cup shredded mozzarella cheese
- · - 1/4 cup cream cheese, softened
- · - 1 teaspoon baking powder
- · - 1 teaspoon Italian seasoning
- · - Salt and pepper, to taste *Toppings:**
- · - 1/2 cup sugar-free pizza sauce
- · - 1 cup shredded mozzarella cheese (for topping)
- · - Pepperoni slices, - Sliced mushrooms
- · - Fresh basil (for garnish)

DIRECTIONS

1. **Preheat the Oven:** Preheat your oven to 350°F (175°C). Line a baking sheet with parchment paper.

2. **Make the Crust:** In a mixing bowl, combine almond flour, egg, mozzarella cheese, cream cheese, baking powder, Italian seasoning, salt, and pepper. Mix until a dough forms. Spread the dough onto the baking sheet, forming a round pizza shape about 1/4 inch thick.

3. **Bake the Crust:** Bake for 15-20 minutes until golden brown.

4. **Add Toppings:** Remove from the oven, spread sugar-free pizza sauce over the crust, and add your desired toppings.

5. **Final Bake:** Return to the oven for another 10-12 minutes until the cheese is melted and bubbly.

6. **Serve:** Let cool slightly, slice, and enjoy.

Keto Portobello Mushroom Pizza

INGREDIENTS

- · - 4 large portobello mushroom caps
- · - 1/2 cup sugar-free pizza sauce
- · - 1 cup shredded mozzarella cheese
- · - Pepperoni slices
- · - Sliced bell peppers
- · - Italian seasoning
- · - Fresh basil or parsley (for garnish)

DIRECTIONS

1. **Preheat the Oven:** Preheat your oven to 375°F (190°C). Line a baking sheet with parchment paper.

2. **Prepare the Mushrooms:** Clean the portobello caps and remove the stems. Place them on the baking sheet, gill side up.

3. **Add Sauce and Toppings:** Spread a tablespoon of pizza sauce in each mushroom cap, then top with shredded mozzarella cheese and your desired toppings.

4. **Bake:** Bake in the preheated oven for about 15-20 minutes, or until the cheese is melted and bubbly.

5. **Serve:** Remove from the oven, garnish with fresh basil or parsley, and enjoy

Keto Almond Flour Cake

INGREDIENTS
- 2 cups almond flour
- - 1/2 cup erythritol (or your preferred keto sweetener)
- - 1/2 cup unsalted butter, softened
- - 4 large eggs
- - 1 teaspoon vanilla extract
- - 1 teaspoon baking powder
- - 1/2 teaspoon salt
- - 1/4 cup unsweetened almond milk (or any low-carb milk)

DIRECTIONS

1. **Preheat the Oven:** Preheat your oven to 350°F (175°C). Grease a 9-inch round cake pan and line the bottom with parchment paper.

2. **Mix Dry Ingredients:** In a bowl, combine almond flour, erythritol, baking powder, and salt.

3. **Cream Butter and Eggs:** In another bowl, beat the softened butter until creamy. Add the eggs one at a time, mixing well after each addition. Stir in the vanilla extract.

4. **Combine Mixtures:** Gradually add the dry ingredients to the wet ingredients, alternating with almond milk, and mix until smooth.

5. **Bake:** Pour the batter into the prepared cake pan and smooth the top. Bake for 25-30 minutes, or until a toothpick inserted in the center comes out clean.

6. **Cool and Serve:** Let the cake cool in the pan for 10 minutes, then transfer it to a wire rack to cool completely. Serve as is or with keto-friendly frosting.

Keto Chocolate Cake

INGREDIENTS
- - 1 1/2 cups almond flour
- - 1/2 cup unsweetened cocoa powder
- - 1/2 cup erythritol (or other sweetener)
- - 1 teaspoon baking powder
- - 1/2 teaspoon baking soda
- - 1/4 teaspoon salt
- - 4 large eggs
- - 1/2 cup unsalted butter, melted
- - 1 teaspoon vanilla extract
- - 1/2 cup unsweetened almond milk

DIRECTIONS

1. **Preheat the Oven:** Preheat your oven to 350°F (175°C). Grease an 8-inch round cake pan and line with parchment paper.

2. **Mix Dry Ingredients:** In a large bowl, whisk together almond flour, cocoa powder, erythritol, baking powder, baking soda, and salt.

3. **Combine Wet Ingredients:** In another bowl, whisk the eggs, melted butter, vanilla extract, and almond milk until well combined.

4. **Combine Mixtures:** Pour the wet ingredients into the dry ingredients and mix until smooth.

5. **Bake:** Pour the batter into the prepared cake pan and bake for 25-30 minutes, or until a toothpick inserted in the center comes out clean.

6. **Cool and Serve:** Allow the cake to cool in the pan for 10 minutes, then transfer to a wire rack to cool completely. Frost with keto-friendly chocolate frosting if desired.

Keto Lemon Cake

INGREDIENTS

- · - 2 cups almond flour
- · - 1/2 cup erythritol (or your preferred sweetener)
- · - 1/2 cup unsalted butter, softened
- · - 4 large eggs
- · - 1/4 cup fresh lemon juice
- · - Zest of 1 lemon
- · - 1 teaspoon baking powder
- · - 1/2 teaspoon salt
- · - 1 teaspoon vanilla extract

DIRECTIONS

1. **Preheat the Oven:** Preheat your oven to 350°F (175°C). Grease a 9-inch round cake pan and line the bottom with parchment paper.
2. **Mix Dry Ingredients:** In a bowl, combine almond flour, erythritol, baking powder, and salt.
3. **Cream Butter and Eggs:** In another bowl, beat the softened butter until creamy. Add the eggs one at a time, mixing well after each addition. Stir in lemon juice, lemon zest, and vanilla extract.
4. **Combine Mixtures:** Gradually add the dry ingredients to the wet ingredients and mix until smooth.
5. **Bake:** Pour the batter into the prepared cake pan and smooth the top. Bake for 25-30 minutes, or until a toothpick inserted in the center comes out clean.
6. **Cool and Serve:** Let the cake cool in the pan for 10 minutes, then transfer it to a wire rack to cool completely. Optionally, top with a sugar-free lemon glaze.

Keto Cheesecake

INGREDIENTS

- · **Ingredients for the Crust:**
- · - 1 1/2 cups almond flour
- · - 1/4 cup erythritol (or your preferred sweetener)
- · - 1/4 cup unsalted butter, melted
- · **Ingredients for the Filling:**
- · - 16 oz (450 g) cream cheese, softened
- · - 1/2 cup erythritol (or other sweetener)
- · - 3 large eggs
- · - 1 teaspoon vanilla extract
- · - 1 tablespoon lemon juice

DIRECTIONS

1. **Preheat the Oven:** Preheat your oven to 325°F (160°C). Grease a 9-inch springform pan.
2. **Prepare the Crust:** In a bowl, mix almond flour, erythritol, and melted butter until combined. Press the mixture into the bottom of the prepared pan.
3. **Bake the Crust:** Bake the crust for 10-12 minutes until lightly golden. Remove from the oven and let cool.
4. **Prepare the Filling:** In a large bowl, beat the cream cheese until smooth. Add erythritol, eggs, vanilla extract, and lemon juice. Mix until well combined and smooth.
5. **Bake the Cheesecake:** Pour the filling over the cooled crust and bake for 45-50 minutes, or until the center is set but still slightly jiggly.
6. **Cool and Serve:** Allow the cheesecake to cool at room temperature, then refrigerate for at least 4 hours (or overnight) before serving. Enjoy plain or with a berry topping.

Stuffed Mushrooms

INGREDIENTS

- · - 12 large portobello or button mushrooms
- · - 8 oz (225 g) cream cheese, softened
- · - 2 cloves garlic, minced
- · - 1 cup fresh spinach, chopped (about 30 g)
- · - 1 cup shredded mozzarella cheese (about 120 g)
- · - 1/4 cup grated Parmesan cheese (about 25 g),1 tsp Italian seasoning
- · - Salt and pepper to taste
- · - 1-2 tbsp olive oil for drizzling

DIRECTIONS

1.Preheat the oven to 375°F (190°C).

2. Clean the mushrooms and remove the stems. Finely chop the stems and set aside.

3. In a skillet, heat a drizzle of olive oil over medium heat. Add the chopped mushroom stems and sauté for 3-4 minutes until soft.

4. Add the minced garlic and chopped spinach to the skillet. Cook until the spinach is wilted, about 2 minutes. Remove from heat and let cool slightly.

5. In a mixing bowl, combine the softened cream cheese, sautéed mixture, mozzarella cheese, Parmesan cheese, Italian seasoning, salt, and pepper. Mix until well combined.

6. Stuff each mushroom cap with the cheese mixture, pressing down gently to pack it in.

7. Place the stuffed mushrooms on a baking sheet. Drizzle with olive oil and bake for 20-25 minutes, or until the tops are golden and bubbly.

8. Serve warm as an appetizer or side dish.

Creamy Mushroom Soup

INGREDIENTS

- · - 1 lb (450 g) mushrooms, sliced (button or cremini)
- · - 1 medium onion, chopped (about 150 g)
- · - 2 cloves garlic, minced
- · - 4 cups (960 ml) vegetable or chicken broth
- · - 1 cup (240 ml) heavy cream
- · - 2 tbsp olive oil or butter, 1 tsp dried thyme
- · - Salt and pepper to taste
- · - Fresh parsley, chopped (for garnish, optional)

DIRECTIONS

1. In a large pot, heat olive oil or butter over medium heat. Add the chopped onions and sauté until translucent, about 5 minutes.

2. Add the minced garlic and sliced mushrooms to the pot. Cook for about 8-10 minutes, stirring occasionally, until the mushrooms are browned and softened.

3. Pour in the broth and add the thyme. Bring to a boil, then reduce the heat and let it simmer for about 15 minutes.

4. Using an immersion blender, blend the soup until smooth. If you don't have an immersion blender, carefully transfer the soup to a regular blender in batches and blend until smooth.

5. Return the blended soup to the pot and stir in the heavy cream. Heat over low heat until warmed through. Season with salt and pepper to taste.

6. Serve hot, garnished with fresh parsley.

Garlic Butter Mushrooms

INGREDIENTS
- · - 1 lb (450 g) whole mushrooms (button or cremini)
- · - 4 tbsp (60 g) unsalted butter
- · - 4 cloves garlic, minced
- · - 1 tsp fresh thyme or 1/2 tsp dried thyme
- · - Salt and pepper to taste
- · - Fresh parsley, chopped (for garnish, optional)

DIRECTIONS

1. Clean the mushrooms with a damp cloth and remove any dirt. Leave them whole.

2. In a large skillet, melt the butter over medium heat. Add the minced garlic and sauté for 1 minute until fragrant, being careful not to burn it.

3. Add the whole mushrooms to the skillet. Cook for about 8-10 minutes, stirring occasionally, until the mushrooms are golden brown and tender.

4. Sprinkle in the thyme, salt, and pepper, stirring to coat the mushrooms evenly.

5. Cook for an additional 2-3 minutes to allow the flavors to meld.

6. Remove from heat and garnish with chopped parsley before serving.

Creamy Chicken and Mushroom Soup

INGREDIENTS
- · - 1 lb (450 g) boneless, skinless chicken thighs or breasts, diced
- · - 8 oz (225 g) mushrooms, sliced (button or cremini)
- · - 1 medium onion, chopped (about 150 g)
- · - 2 cloves garlic, minced
- · - 4 cups (960 ml) chicken broth
- · - 1 cup (240 ml) heavy cream
- · - 2 tbsp olive oil or butter
- · - 1 tsp dried thyme, 1 tsp dried oregano
- · - Salt and pepper to taste
- · - Fresh parsley, chopped (for garnish, optional)

DIRECTIONS

1. In a large pot or Dutch oven, heat the olive oil or butter over medium heat.

2. Add the chopped onion and sauté until translucent, about 5 minutes.

3. Add the diced chicken to the pot and cook until browned on all sides, about 5-7 minutes.

4. Stir in the minced garlic and sliced mushrooms, cooking for another 3-4 minutes until the mushrooms are softened.

5. Pour in the chicken broth, then add the dried thyme, oregano, salt, and pepper. Bring the mixture to a boil.

6. Reduce the heat and let it simmer for about 15-20 minutes, allowing the flavors to meld and the chicken to cook through.

7. Stir in the heavy cream and heat the soup gently until warmed through. Adjust seasoning with additional salt and pepper if needed.

8. Serve hot, garnished with fresh parsley if desired.

Zucchini Noodles with Pesto

INGREDIENTS

- · - 2 medium zucchinis (about 1 lb or 450 g)
- · - 1/2 cup homemade or store-bought pesto
- · - 1/4 cup grated Parmesan cheese
- · - 1 tbsp olive oil
- · - Salt and pepper to taste
- · - Cherry tomatoes for garnish (optional)

DIRECTIONS

1. Spiralize the zucchinis to create noodles. If you don't have a spiralizer, you can use a vegetable peeler to create thin ribbons.

2. Heat olive oil in a skillet over medium heat. Add the zucchini noodles and sauté for 2-3 minutes until just tender.

3. Remove from heat and stir in the pesto until the noodles are well coated. Season with salt and pepper to taste.

4. Serve hot, topped with grated Parmesan cheese and cherry tomatoes if desired.

Cauliflower and Cheese Soup

INGREDIENTS

- · - 1 head cauliflower, chopped into florets (about 4 cups)
- · - 1 medium onion, chopped (about 150 g)
- · - 2 cloves garlic, minced
- · - 4 cups (960 ml) vegetable or chicken broth
- · - 1 cup (240 ml) heavy cream
- · - 1 cup (about 120 g) shredded cheddar cheese
- · - 2 tbsp olive oil or butter
- · - Salt and pepper to taste
- · - Fresh chives or parsley for garnish

DIRECTIONS

1. In a large pot, heat olive oil or butter over medium heat. Add the chopped onion and sauté until translucent, about 5 minutes.

2. Add minced garlic and chopped cauliflower to the pot. Cook for another 3-4 minutes, stirring occasionally.

3. Pour in the broth and bring to a boil. Reduce heat and simmer for about 15-20 minutes, or until the cauliflower is tender.

4. Using an immersion blender, blend the soup until smooth. If you don't have one, carefully transfer to a regular blender in batches.

5. Return the blended soup to the pot, stir in the heavy cream and shredded cheddar cheese. Heat gently until the cheese is melted. Season with salt and pepper.

6. Serve hot, garnished with fresh chives or parsley if desired.

Spinach and Artichoke Dip

INGREDIENTS

- · - 1 cup frozen spinach, thawed and drained
- · - 1 cup canned artichoke hearts, chopped
- · - 8 oz (225 g) cream cheese, softened
- · - 1/2 cup sour cream
- · - 1/2 cup grated Parmesan cheese
- · - 1 cup shredded mozzarella cheese

- · - 2 cloves garlic, minced
- · - Salt and pepper to taste
- · - Olive oil for greasing

DIRECTIONS

1. Preheat the oven to 375°F (190°C). Grease a baking dish with olive oil.

2. In a mixing bowl, combine the softened cream cheese, sour cream, chopped artichokes, thawed spinach, minced garlic, Parmesan cheese, salt, and pepper. Mix until well combined.

3. Transfer the mixture to the greased baking dish and spread evenly. Top with shredded mozzarella cheese.

4. Bake for 20-25 minutes, or until the cheese is melted and bubbly.

5. Serve warm with veggie sticks or keto-friendly crackers.

Zucchini Noodles with Alfredo Sauce

INGREDIENTS

- · - 2 medium zucchinis (about 1 lb or 450 g), spiralized
- · - 1 cup heavy cream (240 ml)
- · - 1/2 cup grated Parmesan cheese (about 50 g)
- · - 2 cloves garlic, minced
- · - 2 tbsp butter
- · - Salt and pepper to taste
- · - Fresh parsley for garnish

DIRECTIONS

. Spiralize the zucchinis to create noodles.

2. In a skillet, melt the butter over medium heat. Add the minced garlic and sauté for about 1 minute until fragrant.

3. Pour in the heavy cream and bring to a gentle simmer. Stir in the Parmesan cheese until melted and smooth. Season with salt and pepper.

4. Add the zucchini noodles to the skillet and toss to coat in the sauce. Cook for 2-3 minutes until the noodles are slightly tender.

5. Serve immediately, garnished with fresh parsley if desired.

Spaghetti Squash with Meat Sauce

INGREDIENTS

- · - 1 medium spaghetti squash
- · - 1 lb (450 g) ground beef or turkey
- · - 1 can (14 oz) diced tomatoes
- · - 1 small onion, chopped
- · - 2 cloves garlic, minced
- · - 1 tsp dried Italian seasoning
- · - Salt and pepper to taste
- · - Olive oil for cooking
- · - Fresh basil for garnish

DIRECTIONS

1. Preheat the oven to 400°F (200°C). Cut the spaghetti squash in half lengthwise and scoop out the seeds. Drizzle with olive oil and season with salt and pepper.

2. Place the squash cut-side down on a baking sheet and roast for about 30-40 minutes, or until tender.

3. In a skillet, heat olive oil over medium heat. Add the chopped onion and sauté until translucent, about 5 minutes. Add the minced garlic and cook for another minute.

4. Add the ground meat to the skillet and cook until browned. Stir in the diced tomatoes and Italian seasoning. Simmer for about 10 minutes, seasoning with salt and pepper.

5. Once the spaghetti squash is cooked, use a fork to scrape out the strands. Serve topped with the meat sauce and garnish with fresh basil if desired.

Keto Lasagna with Zucchini

INGREDIENTS

- · - 2 large zucchinis, sliced lengthwise into thin strips
- · - 1 lb (450 g) ground beef or Italian sausage
- · - 1 can (14 oz) crushed tomatoes
- · - 1 cup ricotta cheese (240 g),1 egg
- · - 2 cups shredded mozzarella cheese (about 240 g)
- · - 1 tsp dried oregano
- · - 1 tsp dried basil
- · - Salt and pepper to taste
- · - Olive oil for cooking

DIRECTIONS

. Preheat the oven to 375°F (190°C).

2. In a skillet, heat olive oil over medium heat. Add the ground meat and cook until browned. Stir in the crushed tomatoes, oregano, basil, salt, and pepper. Simmer for about 10 minutes.

3. In a bowl, mix the ricotta cheese with the egg, salt, and pepper.

4. In a baking dish, spread a layer of the meat sauce, followed by a layer of zucchini strips, then a layer of the ricotta mixture. Repeat the layers, finishing with a layer of meat sauce on top.

5. Sprinkle the shredded mozzarella cheese evenly over the top.

6. Cover the dish with aluminum foil and bake for 25 minutes. Remove the foil and bake for an additional 15 minutes or until the cheese is bubbly and golden.

7. Let cool for a few minutes before slicing and serving.

Keto Chocolate Chip Cookies

INGREDIENTS

- · - 2 cups almond flour (about 200 g)
- · - 1/2 cup erythritol or your preferred keto sweetener
- · - 1/2 cup unsalted butter, softened (about 115 g)
- · - 1 large egg
- · - 1 tsp vanilla extract
- · - 1/2 tsp baking soda
- · - 1/4 tsp salt
- · - 1/2 cup sugar-free chocolate chips (about 90 g)

DIRECTIONS

1. Preheat the oven to 350°F (175°C) and line a baking sheet with parchment paper.

2. In a mixing bowl, cream together the softened butter and erythritol until light and fluffy.

3. Add the egg and vanilla extract, mixing until well combined.

4. In another bowl, whisk together the almond flour, baking soda, and salt. Gradually add this dry mixture to the wet ingredients, stirring until a dough forms.

5. Fold in the sugar-free chocolate chips.

6. Scoop tablespoon-sized portions of dough onto the prepared baking sheet, spacing them about 2 inches apart.

7. Bake for 12-15 minutes, or until the edges are golden. Allow to cool on the baking sheet for a few minutes before transferring to a wire rack to cool completely.

Keto Peanut Butter Cookies

INGREDIENTS

- , - 1 cup natural peanut butter (about 250 g)
- - 1/2 cup erythritol or your preferred keto sweetener
- - 1 large egg
- - 1 tsp vanilla extract
- - 1/2 tsp baking soda
- - 1/4 tsp salt

DIRECTIONS

1. Preheat the oven to 350°F (175°C) and line a baking sheet with parchment paper.
2. In a mixing bowl, combine the peanut butter, erythritol, egg, vanilla extract, baking soda, and salt. Mix until well combined.
3. Scoop tablespoon-sized portions of dough and roll them into balls. Place them on the prepared baking sheet and press down with a fork to create a crisscross pattern.
4. Bake for 10-12 minutes, or until the edges are set and slightly golden. Let cool on the baking sheet for a few minutes before transferring to a wire rack to cool completely.

Keto Snickerdoodle Cookies

INGREDIENTS

- - 2 cups almond flour (about 200 g)
- - 1/2 cup erythritol or your preferred keto sweetener
- - 1/2 cup unsalted butter, softened (about 115 g)
- - 1 large egg
- - 1 tsp vanilla extract
- - 1/2 tsp baking powder
- - 1/2 tsp cinnamon,1/4 tsp salt
- **For the Cinnamon Sugar Coating:**
- - 1 tbsp erythritol or keto sweetener
- - 1 tsp cinnamon

DIRECTIONS

1. Preheat the oven to 350°F (175°C) and line a baking sheet with parchment paper.
2. In a mixing bowl, cream together the softened butter and erythritol until light and fluffy.
3. Add the egg and vanilla extract, mixing until well combined.
4. In another bowl, whisk together the almond flour, baking powder, cinnamon, and salt. Gradually add this dry mixture to the wet ingredients, stirring until a dough forms.
5. In a small bowl, combine the erythritol and cinnamon for the coating.
6. Scoop tablespoon-sized portions of dough and roll them into balls. Roll each ball in the cinnamon-sugar mixture and place them on the prepared baking sheet, spacing them about 2 inches apart.
7. Bake for 10-12 minutes, or until the edges are set. Let cool on the baking sheet for a few minutes before transferring to a wire rack to cool completely.

Classic Keto Chicken Salad

INGREDIENTS

- - 2 cups cooked chicken, shredded or diced (about 300 g)
- - 1/2 cup mayonnaise (120 ml)
- - 1/4 cup celery, chopped (about 30 g)
- - 1/4 cup red onion, finely chopped (about 30 g)
- - 1 tbsp Dijon mustard

- · - 1 tbsp lemon juice
- · - Salt and pepper to taste
- · - Lettuce leaves for serving

DIRECTIONS

1. In a large mixing bowl, combine the shredded chicken, mayonnaise, chopped celery, red onion, Dijon mustard, and lemon juice.

2. Mix well until all ingredients are combined. Season with salt and pepper to taste.

3. Serve on a bed of lettuce or enjoy on its own. Store any leftovers in an airtight container in the refrigerator.

Avocado Chicken Salad

INGREDIENTS

- · - 2 cups cooked chicken, shredded or diced (about 300g)
- · - 1 ripe avocado, mashed
- · - 1/4 cup mayonnaise (120 ml)
- · - 1/4 cup cilantro, chopped (optional)
- · - 1 lime, juiced
- · - 1/4 cup red onion, finely chopped (about 30 g)
- · - Salt and pepper to taste
- · - Cherry tomatoes for garnish

DIRECTIONS

1. In a large bowl, combine the shredded chicken, mashed avocado, mayonnaise, chopped cilantro, lime juice, and red onion.

2. Mix until well combined and creamy. Season with salt and pepper to taste.

3. Serve immediately, garnished with cherry tomatoes if desired. This salad is great on its own or wrapped in lettuce.

Creamy Pesto Chicken Salad

INGREDIENTS

- · - 2 cups cooked chicken, shredded or diced (about 300 g)
- · - 1/2 cup mayonnaise (120 ml)
- · - 1/4 cup pesto (store-bought or homemade)
- · - 1/4 cup cherry tomatoes, halved
- · - 1/4 cup mozzarella cheese, diced (optional)
- · - Salt and pepper to taste
- · - Fresh basil for garnish

DIRECTIONS

1. In a large mixing bowl, combine the shredded chicken, mayonnaise, and pesto. Mix until well combined.

2. Gently fold in the halved cherry tomatoes and diced mozzarella cheese.

3. Season with salt and pepper to taste.

4. Serve chilled, garnished with fresh basil if desired. This salad is perfect for meal prep or as a quick lunch option.

Keto Almond Flour Pancakes

INGREDIENTS

- · - 1 cup almond flour (about 100 g)
- · - 2 large eggs
- · - 1/4 cup unsweetened almond milk (60 ml)
- · - 1 tbsp erythritol or your preferred keto sweetener
- · - 1 tsp baking powder
- · - 1/2 tsp vanilla extract, - Pinch of salt, - Butter or coconut oil for cooking

DIRECTIONS

1. In a mixing bowl, combine almond flour, erythritol, baking powder, and salt.

2. In another bowl, whisk together the eggs, almond milk, and vanilla extract.

3. Pour the wet ingredients into the dry ingredients and mix until well combined.

4. Heat a skillet over medium heat and add butter or coconut oil.

5. Pour about 1/4 cup of the batter for each pancake onto the skillet. Cook for 2-3 minutes until bubbles form on the surface, then flip and cook for another 2-3 minutes until golden.

6. Serve warm with sugar-free syrup or fresh berries.

Keto Chocolate Chip Cookies

INGREDIENTS

- · - 2 cups almond flour (about 200 g)
- · - 1/2 cup erythritol or your preferred keto sweetener
- · - 1/2 cup unsalted butter, softened (about 115 g)
- · - 1 large egg
- · - 1 tsp vanilla extract
- · - 1/2 tsp baking soda
- · - 1/4 tsp salt
- · - 1/2 cup sugar-free chocolate chips (about 90 g)

DIRECTIONS

1. Preheat the oven to 350°F (175°C) and line a baking sheet with parchment paper.

2. In a mixing bowl, cream together the softened butter and erythritol until light and fluffy.

3. Add the egg and vanilla extract, mixing until well combined.

4. In another bowl, whisk together the almond flour, baking soda, and salt. Gradually add this dry mixture to the wet ingredients, stirring until a dough forms.

5. Fold in the sugar-free chocolate chips.

6. Scoop tablespoon-sized portions of dough onto the prepared baking sheet, spacing them about 2 inches apart.

7. Bake for 12-15 minutes, or until the edges are golden. Allow to cool on the baking sheet for a few minutes before transferring to a wire rack.

Keto Berry Crumble

INGREDIENTS

- · - 2 cups mixed berries (fresh or frozen, such as blueberries, raspberries, or strawberries)
- · - 1/4 cup erythritol or your preferred keto sweetener
- · - 1 tbsp lemon juice
- · - 1 cup almond flour (about 100 g)
- · - 1/2 cup unsalted butter, melted (about 115 g)
- · - 1/2 tsp cinnamon
- · - Pinch of salt

DIRECTIONS

1. Preheat the oven to 350°F (175°C) and grease a baking dish.
2. In a bowl, combine the mixed berries, erythritol, and lemon juice. Spread the mixture evenly in the bottom of the greased baking dish.
3. In another bowl, mix the almond flour, melted butter, cinnamon, and salt until crumbly.
4. Sprinkle the almond flour mixture over the berry layer.
5. Bake for 25-30 minutes, or until the topping is golden and the berries are bubbly.
6. Serve warm, optionally with a dollop of whipped cream or sugar-free ice cream.

Tuna Avocado Salad

INGREDIENTS

- · -1 can (5 oz or 140 g) tuna, drained
- · - 1 ripe avocado, diced
- · - 1/4 cup mayonnaise (60 ml)
- · - 1 tbsp lemon juice
- · - 1/4 cup celery, chopped (about 30 g)
- · - 1/4 cup red onion, finely chopped (about 30 g)
- · - Salt and pepper to taste
- · - Lettuce leaves for serving (optiona)

DIRECTIONS

1. In a mixing bowl, combine the drained tuna, diced avocado, mayonnaise, lemon juice, chopped celery, and red onion.
2. Mix gently until well combined. Season with salt and pepper to taste.
3. Serve immediately on a bed of lettuce or enjoy on its own.

Salmon Salad with Dill Dressing

INGREDIENTS

- · - 1 can (5 oz or 140 g) salmon, drained (or 1 cup cooked salmon, flaked)
- · - 2 cups mixed greens (such as spinach, arugula, or romaine)
- · - 1/4 cup cucumber, diced
- · - 1/4 cup cherry tomatoes, halved
- · - 1/4 cup red onion, thinly sliced (optional)
- · **For the Dill Dressing:**
- · - 1/4 cup mayonnaise (60 ml)
- · - 1 tbsp lemon juice
- · - 1 tbsp fresh dill, chopped (or 1 tsp dried dill),Salt and pepper to taste

DIRECTIONS

1. In a small bowl, whisk together the mayonnaise, lemon juice, dill, salt, and pepper to make the dressing.
2. In a large bowl, combine the salmon, mixed greens, cucumber, cherry tomatoes, and red onion.
3. Drizzle the dill dressing over the salad and toss gently to combine.
4. Serve immediately.

Shrimp and Avocado Salad

INGREDIENTS

- · - 1 lb (450 g) cooked shrimp, peeled and deveined
- · - 1 ripe avocado, diced
- · - 1/4 cup red onion, finely chopped (about 30 g)
- · - 1/4 cup cilantro, chopped (optional)
- · - 1 lime, juiced
- · - 2 tbsp olive oil
- · - Salt and pepper to taste
- · - Lettuce leaves for serving (optional)

DIRECTIONS

1. In a large mixing bowl, combine the cooked shrimp, diced avocado, red onion, and cilantro.
2. In a small bowl, whisk together the lime juice, olive oil, salt, and pepper.
3. Pour the dressing over the shrimp mixture and toss gently to coat.
4. Serve on a bed of lettuce leaves or on its own.

Cheesy Cauliflower Casserole

INGREDIENTS

- · -1 head cauliflower, cut into florets (about 4 cups)
- · - 1 cup shredded cheddar cheese (about 120 g)
- · - 1/2 cup cream cheese (about 115 g), softened
- · - 1/2 cup heavy cream (120 ml)
- · - 1/4 cup grated Parmesan cheese (25 g)
- · - 2 cloves garlic, minced
- · - 1/2 tsp onion powder
- · - Salt and pepper to taste
- · - 1/4 cup green onions, chopped (for garnish)

DIRECTIONS

1. Preheat the oven to 375°F (190°C).
2. Steam the cauliflower florets until tender, about 5-7 minutes. Drain well and let cool slightly.
3. In a mixing bowl, combine the cheddar cheese, cream cheese, heavy cream, Parmesan cheese, minced garlic, onion powder, salt, and pepper. Mix until smooth.
4. Fold in the steamed cauliflower until well coated.
5. Transfer the mixture to a greased baking dish and spread evenly.
6. Bake for 25-30 minutes, or until bubbly and golden on top. Garnish with chopped green onions before serving.

Keto Chicken Alfredo Bake

INGREDIENTS

- · - 2 cups cooked chicken, shredded or diced (about 300 g)
- · - 1 cup heavy cream (240 ml)
- · - 1/2 cup grated Parmesan cheese (50 g)
- · - 1 cup broccoli florets (fresh or frozen)
- · - 2 cups cauliflower rice (about 300 g)
- · - 2 cloves garlic, minced
- · - 1 tsp Italian seasoning
- · - Salt and pepper to taste
- · - 1 cup shredded mozzarella cheese (about 120 g)

DIRECTIONS

1. Preheat the oven to 375°F (190°C) and grease a baking dish.

2. In a mixing bowl, combine the heavy cream, Parmesan cheese, minced garlic, Italian seasoning, salt, and pepper.

3. In the prepared baking dish, layer the cauliflower rice, followed by the shredded chicken and broccoli florets.

4. Pour the cream mixture over the top and mix gently to combine.

5. Sprinkle shredded mozzarella cheese on top.

6. Bake for 25-30 minutes, or until the cheese is melted and bubbly. Let cool slightly before serving.

Zucchini Lasagna

INGREDIENTS

- · - 3 medium zucchinis, sliced lengthwise into thin strips
- · - 1 lb (450 g) ground beef or Italian sausage
- · - 1 can (14 oz) crushed tomatoes
- · - 1/2 cup ricotta cheese (120 g)
- · - 1 cup shredded mozzarella cheese (about 120 g)
- · - 1/4 cup grated Parmesan cheese (25 g)
- · - 1 tsp Italian seasoning
- · - Salt and pepper to taste
- · - Olive oil for cooking

DIRECTIONS

1. Preheat the oven to 375°F (190°C).

2. In a skillet, heat olive oil over medium heat. Add the ground beef or sausage, cooking until browned. Drain excess fat.

3. Stir in the crushed tomatoes, Italian seasoning, salt, and pepper. Simmer for about 10 minutes.

4. In a baking dish, spread a layer of the meat sauce on the bottom. Layer half of the zucchini slices on top, followed by half of the ricotta cheese. Repeat the layers with the remaining ingredients, finishing with the meat sauce.

5. Top with shredded mozzarella and grated Parmesan cheese.

6. Cover with aluminum foil and bake for 25 minutes. Remove the foil and bake for an additional 15 minutes, or until the cheese is bubbly and golden.

7. Let cool for a few minutes before slicing and serving.

Avocado Egg Salad

INGREDIENTS

- · - 2 ripe avocados, diced
- · - 4 hard-boiled eggs, chopped
- · - 1/4 cup mayonnaise (60 ml)
- · - 1 tbsp Dijon mustard
- · - 1 tbsp lemon juice
- · - Salt and pepper to taste
- · - Lettuce leaves for serving (optional)

DIRECTIONS

1. In a mixing bowl, combine the diced avocados and chopped hard-boiled eggs.

2. Add the mayonnaise, Dijon mustard, lemon juice, salt, and pepper. Gently mix until well combined.

3. Serve on a bed of lettuce leaves or enjoy on its own.

Keto Avocado Chicken Salad

INGREDIENTS
- · - 2 cups cooked chicken, shredded or diced (about 300 g)
- · - 1 ripe avocado, mashed
- · - 1/4 cup mayonnaise (60 ml), 1 tbsp lime juice,1/4 cup celery, chopped (about 30 g)
- · - 1/4 cup red onion, finely chopped (about 30 g)
- · - Salt and pepper to taste
- · - Fresh cilantro for garnish (optional)

DIRECTIONS

1. In a large mixing bowl, combine the shredded chicken, mashed avocado, mayonnaise, lime juice, chopped celery, and red onion.

2. Mix well until all ingredients are combined. Season with salt and pepper to taste.

3. Serve chilled, garnished with fresh cilantro if desired.

Grilled Avocado with Shrimp

INGREDIENTS
- · - 2 ripe avocados, halved and pitted
- · - 1 lb (450 g) shrimp, peeled and deveined
- · - 2 tbsp olive oil
- · - 1 tsp garlic powder
- · - 1 tsp paprika
- · - Salt and pepper to taste
- · - Lime wedges for serving

DIRECTIONS

1. Preheat the grill to medium heat.

2. In a bowl, toss the shrimp with olive oil, garlic powder, paprika, salt, and pepper until well coated.

3. Place the avocado halves, cut side down, on the grill for about 3-4 minutes until grill marks appear.

4. While the avocados are grilling, grill the shrimp for about 2-3 minutes on each side, until pink and cooked through.

5. Remove the avocados and shrimp from the grill. Fill the avocado halves with the grilled shrimp.

6. Serve with lime wedges for squeezing over the top.

Keto Egg Muffins

INGREDIENTS
- · - 6 large eggs
- · - 1/2 cup heavy cream (120 ml)
- · - 1/2 cup bell peppers, diced
- · - 1/2 cup spinach, chopped
- · - 1/4 cup onion, finely chopped
- · - 1/2 cup shredded cheese (cheddar, mozzarella, or your choice)
- · - Salt and pepper to taste
- · - Olive oil or cooking spray for greasing

DIRECTIONS

1. Preheat the oven to 350°F (175°C) and grease a muffin tin.

2. In a mixing bowl, whisk together the eggs and heavy cream until well combined.

3. Stir in the bell peppers, spinach, onion, cheese, salt, and pepper.

4. Pour the egg mixture evenly into the muffin tin, filling each cup about 3/4 full.

5. Bake for 18-20 minutes, or until the egg muffins are set and slightly golden.

6. Allow to cool for a few minutes before removing from the tin. Serve warm or store in the fridge for meal prep.

Keto Shakshuka

INGREDIENTS
- · - 2 tbsp olive oil
- · - 1 onion, diced
- · - 1 bell pepper, diced
- · - 3 cloves garlic, minced
- · - 1 can (14 oz or 400 g) diced tomatoes
- · - 1 tsp cumin
- · - 1 tsp paprika
- · - Salt and pepper to taste
- · - 4 large eggs
- · - Fresh parsley or cilantro for garnish

DIRECTIONS
1. In a large skillet, heat olive oil over medium heat. Add the onion and bell pepper, cooking until softened, about 5 minutes.
2. Stir in the garlic and cook for an additional minute until fragrant.
3. Add the diced tomatoes, cumin, paprika, salt, and pepper. Simmer for about 10 minutes, allowing the sauce to thicken.
4. Create small wells in the sauce and crack an egg into each well. Cover the skillet and cook for 5-7 minutes, or until the egg whites are set but the yolks are still runny.
5. Remove from heat and garnish with fresh parsley or cilantro. Serve warm.

Keto Cloud Eggs

INGREDIENTS
- · - 4 large eggs
- · - Salt and pepper to taste
- · - 1/4 cup shredded cheese (cheddar, mozzarella, or your choice)
- · - Optional toppings: chives, bacon bits, or herbs

DIRECTIONS
1. Preheat the oven to 450°F (230°C) and line a baking sheet with parchment paper.
2. Separate the egg whites from the yolks, placing the whites in a mixing bowl and the yolks in separate small bowls.
3. Using an electric mixer, beat the egg whites until stiff peaks form.
4. Gently fold in the shredded cheese, salt, and pepper.
5. Scoop the whipped egg whites onto the prepared baking sheet, forming nests with a well in the center for the yolk.
6. Carefully place a yolk in each egg white nest.
7. Bake for 5-7 minutes, or until the egg whites are golden and the yolks are set to your liking.
8. Remove from the oven and add any optional toppings before serving.

Keto Pork Chops with Garlic Butter

INGREDIENTS

- · - 4 bone-in pork chops (about 1 inch thick)
- · - Salt and pepper to taste
- · - 2 tbsp olive oil
- · - 4 tbsp unsalted butter
- · - 4 cloves garlic, minced
- · - 1 tsp fresh rosemary, chopped (or 1/2 tsp dried)
- · - 1 tsp fresh thyme, chopped (or 1/2 tsp dried)

DIRECTIONS

1. Season the pork chops generously with salt and pepper on both sides.
2. In a large skillet, heat the olive oil over medium-high heat. Add the pork chops and sear for about 4-5 minutes on each side until golden brown and cooked through. Remove from the skillet and set aside.
3. In the same skillet, reduce heat to medium and add the butter, minced garlic, rosemary, and thyme. Cook for 1-2 minutes until fragrant.
4. Return the pork chops to the skillet and spoon the garlic butter over them. Cook for an additional 1-2 minutes to heat through.
5. Serve the pork chops drizzled with the garlic butter sauce.

Keto Pulled Pork

INGREDIENTS

- · - 3 lb (1.4 kg) pork shoulder (also known as pork butt)
- · - 1 cup low-sugar BBQ sauce (check for keto-friendly options)
- · - 1 tbsp smoked paprika
- · - 1 tbsp garlic powder
- · - 1 tbsp onion powder
- · - Salt and pepper to taste
- · - 1/2 cup chicken broth

DIRECTIONS

1. Preheat the oven to 300°F (150°C).
2. In a small bowl, mix together the smoked paprika, garlic powder, onion powder, salt, and pepper. Rub the spice mixture all over the pork shoulder.
3. Place the pork shoulder in a roasting pan and pour the chicken broth around it.
4. Cover the pan tightly with aluminum foil and roast in the oven for about 4-5 hours or until the pork is tender and easily shreds with a fork.
5. Remove the pork from the oven and let it rest for about 15 minutes. Shred the meat using two forks and mix with the low-sugar BBQ sauce.
6. Serve warm, either on its own or with a side of keto-friendly coleslaw.

Keto Stuffed Pork Tenderloin

INGREDIENTS

- · - 1 lb (450 g) pork tenderloin
- · - 1/2 cup spinach, chopped
- · - 1/2 cup cream cheese (about 120 g), softened
- · - 1/2 cup feta cheese, crumbled
- · - 1/4 cup sun-dried tomatoes, chopped
- · - 1 tsp garlic powder
- · - Salt and pepper to taste

· - Olive oil for drizzling

DIRECTIONS

1. Season the pork chops generously with salt and pepper on both sides.

2. In a large skillet, heat the olive oil over medium-high heat. Add the pork chops and sear for about 4-5 minutes on each side until golden brown and cooked through. Remove from the skillet and set aside.

3. In the same skillet, reduce heat to medium and add the butter, minced garlic, rosemary, and thyme. Cook for 1-2 minutes until fragrant.

4. Return the pork chops to the skillet and spoon the garlic butter over them. Cook for an additional 1-2 minutes to heat through.

5. Serve the pork chops drizzled with the garlic butter sauce.

Keto Pulled Pork

INGREDIENTS

· - 1 lb (450 g) pork tenderloin
· - 1/2 cup spinach, chopped
· - 1/2 cup cream cheese (about 120 g), softened
· - 1/2 cup feta cheese, crumbled
· - 1/4 cup sun-dried tomatoes, chopped
· - 1 tsp garlic powder
· - Salt and pepper to taste
· - Olive oil for drizzling

DIRECTIONS

1. Preheat the oven to 375°F (190°C).

2. In a mixing bowl, combine the chopped spinach, cream cheese, feta cheese, sun-dried tomatoes, garlic powder, salt, and pepper. Mix until well combined.

3. Using a sharp knife, carefully cut a slit down the center of the pork tenderloin, creating a pocket for the filling. Be careful not to cut all the way through.

4. Stuff the pork tenderloin with the cheese and spinach mixture.

5. Place the stuffed tenderloin in a baking dish, drizzle with olive oil, and season with salt and pepper.

6. Bake for 25-30 minutes or until the pork is cooked through and reaches an internal temperature of 145°F (63°C).

7. Let rest for a few minutes before slicing and serving.

Creamy Kale and Mushroom Soup

INGREDIENTS

· - 1 tbsp olive oil
· - 1 onion, diced
· - 2 cloves garlic, minced
· - 8 oz (225 g) mushrooms, sliced
· - 4 cups kale, chopped
· - 4 cups chicken or vegetable broth (960 ml)
· - 1 cup heavy cream (240 ml)
· - Salt and pepper to taste
· - 1/4 cup grated Parmesan cheese (optional)

DIRECTIONS

1. In a large pot, heat the olive oil over medium heat. Add the diced onion and cook until softened, about 5 minutes.

2. Add the minced garlic and sliced mushrooms, cooking for an additional 5 minutes until the mushrooms are tender.

3. Stir in the chopped kale and cook until wilted.

4. Pour in the broth and bring to a simmer. Let it cook for about 10 minutes.

5. Reduce the heat and stir in the heavy cream. Season with salt and pepper.

6. If using, stir in the grated Parmesan cheese before serving. Enjoy warm!

Kale Salad with Lemon Vinaigrette

INGREDIENTS

- · - 4 cups kale, stems removed and leaves chopped
- · - 1/4 cup olive oil
- · - 2 tbsp lemon juice
- · - 1 tsp Dijon mustard
- · - 1/2 tsp garlic powder
- · - Salt and pepper to taste
- · - 1/4 cup walnuts or pecans, chopped
- · - 1/4 cup feta cheese, crumbled (optional)

DIRECTIONS

1. In a small bowl, whisk together the olive oil, lemon juice, Dijon mustard, garlic powder, salt, and pepper to create the vinaigrette.

2. In a large bowl, add the chopped kale. Drizzle with the vinaigrette and massage the kale leaves with your hands for about 2-3 minutes until they soften.

3. Toss in the chopped walnuts or pecans and feta cheese, if using.

4. Serve immediately or let it sit for a few minutes to allow the flavors to meld.

Baked Kale Chips

INGREDIENTS

- · - 4 cups kale, stems removed and leaves torn into bite-sized pieces
- · - 2 tbsp olive oil
- · - 1/2 tsp garlic powder
- · - 1/2 tsp smoked paprika (or your favorite seasoning)
- · - Salt to taste

DIRECTIONS

1. Preheat the oven to 350°F (175°C) and line a baking sheet with parchment paper.

2. In a large bowl, toss the kale pieces with olive oil, garlic powder, smoked paprika, and salt until evenly coated.

3. Spread the kale in a single layer on the prepared baking sheet.

4. Bake for 10-15 minutes, or until the edges are crispy, checking frequently to prevent burning.

5. Let cool slightly before serving as a crunchy snack or side dish.

Keto Cauliflower Mash

INGREDIENTS

- · - 1 head of cauliflower, cut into florets
- · - 1/4 cup unsalted butter (about 60 g)
- · - 1/4 cup heavy cream (60 ml)
- · - 1/2 tsp garlic powder
- · - Salt and pepper to taste
- · - Chives or parsley for garnish (optional)

DIRECTIONS

1. Steam the cauliflower florets until tender, about 10-15 minutes.

2. Drain any excess water and transfer the cauliflower to a mixing bowl.

3. Add the butter, heavy cream, garlic powder, salt, and pepper. Mash with a potato masher or use an immersion blender for a smoother texture.

4. Adjust seasoning to taste, and garnish with chopped chives or parsley if desired. Serve warm.

Keto Radish "Potato" Salad

INGREDIENTS

- · - 1 lb (450 g) radishes, trimmed and halved
- · - 1/4 cup mayonnaise (60 ml)
- · - 1 tbsp Dijon mustard
- · - 2 tbsp apple cider vinegar
- · - 1/4 cup celery, chopped
- · - 1/4 cup green onions, chopped
- · - Salt and pepper to taste
- · - Fresh dill or parsley for garnish (optional)

DIRECTIONS

1. Preheat the oven to 400°F (200°C). Toss the radishes with olive oil, salt, and pepper, and spread them on a baking sheet.

2. Roast for about 20-25 minutes, or until tender and slightly caramelized. Let them cool.

3. In a mixing bowl, combine the mayonnaise, Dijon mustard, apple cider vinegar, chopped celery, and green onions.

4. Once the radishes have cooled, add them to the bowl and mix gently to combine.

5. Adjust seasoning to taste, and garnish with fresh dill or parsley if desired. Serve chilled or at room temperature.

Cheesy Cauliflower Casserole

INGREDIENTS

- · - 1 head cauliflower, cut into florets (about 4 cups)
- · - 1 cup shredded cheddar cheese (about 120 g)
- · - 1/2 cup cream cheese (about 115 g), softened
- · - 1/4 cup heavy cream (60 ml)
- · - 1/2 tsp garlic powder
- · - Salt and pepper to taste
- · - 1/4 cup grated Parmesan cheese (optional)

DIRECTIONS

1. Preheat the oven to 375°F (190°C) and grease a baking dish.

2. Steam the cauliflower florets until tender, about 5-7 minutes. Drain well and let cool slightly.

3. In a mixing bowl, combine the cheddar cheese, cream cheese, heavy cream, garlic powder, salt, and pepper. Mix until smooth.

4. Fold in the steamed cauliflower until well coated.

5. Transfer the mixture to the prepared baking dish and top with grated Parmesan cheese if desired.

6. Bake for 25-30 minutes, or until bubbly and golden on top. Let cool slightly before serving.

Cheesy Cauliflower Bake

INGREDIENTS

- -1 head cauliflower, cut into florets
- - 1 cup shredded cheddar cheese (about 120 g)
- - 1/2 cup cream cheese (about 115 g), softened
- - 1/4 cup heavy cream (60 ml)
- - 1/4 cup grated Parmesan cheese (25 g)
- - 1 tsp garlic powder
- - Salt and pepper to taste
- - Fresh parsley for garnish (optional)

DIRECTIONS

1. Preheat the oven to 375°F (190°C) and grease a baking dish.
2. Steam the cauliflower florets until tender, about 5-7 minutes. Drain well and let cool slightly.
3. In a mixing bowl, combine the cheddar cheese, cream cheese, heavy cream, garlic powder, salt, and pepper. Mix until smooth.
4. Fold in the steamed cauliflower until well coated.
5. Transfer the mixture to the prepared baking dish and top with grated Parmesan cheese.
6. Bake for 25-30 minutes, or until bubbly and golden on top. Garnish with fresh parsley before serving.

Keto Cheese Crisps

INGREDIENTS

- - 1 cup shredded cheese (cheddar, Parmesan, or your choice)
- - Optional seasonings: garlic powder, Italian seasoning, or paprika

DIRECTIONS

1. Preheat the oven to 400°F (200°C) and line a baking sheet with parchment paper.
2. In a bowl, mix the shredded cheese with any optional seasonings.
3. Drop tablespoon-sized mounds of the cheese mixture onto the prepared baking sheet, spacing them apart.
4. Bake for 5-7 minutes, or until the cheese is melted and bubbly, and the edges are golden.
5. Allow to cool for a few minutes before removing them from the parchment paper. Enjoy as a snack or topping for salads!

Spinach and Cheese Stuffed Chicken Breast

INGREDIENTS

- - 2 large chicken breasts
- - 1 cup fresh spinach, chopped
- - 1/2 cup cream cheese (about 115 g), softened
- - 1/2 cup shredded mozzarella cheese (about 60 g)
- - 1/4 cup grated Parmesan cheese (25 g)
- - 1 clove garlic, minced
- - Salt and pepper to taste
- - Olive oil for drizzling

DIRECTIONS

1. Preheat the oven to 375°F (190°C) and grease a baking dish.
2. In a mixing bowl, combine the chopped spinach, cream cheese, mozzarella cheese, grated Parmesan cheese, minced garlic, salt, and pepper. Mix until well combined.
3. Carefully slice a pocket into each chicken breast and stuff with the cheese and spinach mixture.

4. Place the stuffed chicken breasts in the baking dish, drizzle with olive oil, and season with salt and pepper.

5. Bake for 25-30 minutes, or until the chicken is cooked through and reaches an internal temperature of 165°F (75°C). Let rest for a few minutes before serving.

Roasted Garlic Butter Carrots

INGREDIENTS
- · - 2 cups baby carrots (or sliced regular carrots)
- · - 3 tbsp unsalted butter, melted
- · - 3 cloves garlic, minced
- · - 1 tsp dried thyme (or fresh thyme)
- · - Salt and pepper to taste
- · - Fresh parsley for garnish (optional)

DIRECTIONS

1. Preheat the oven to 400°F (200°C) and line a baking sheet with parchment paper.

2. In a mixing bowl, combine the melted butter, minced garlic, thyme, salt, and pepper.

3. Add the carrots to the bowl and toss until they are well coated with the garlic butter mixture.

4. Spread the carrots in a single layer on the prepared baking sheet.

5. Roast for 20-25 minutes, or until tender and slightly caramelized, tossing halfway through.

6. Garnish with fresh parsley before serving.

Keto Carrot and Zucchini Fritters

INGREDIENTS
- · - 1 cup grated carrots
- · - 1 cup grated zucchini (squeeze out excess moisture)
- · - 1/4 cup almond flour
- · - 2 large eggs
- · - 1/4 cup grated Parmesan cheese
- · - 1 tsp garlic powder
- · - Salt and pepper to taste
- · - Olive oil for frying

DIRECTIONS

1. In a large mixing bowl, combine the grated carrots, grated zucchini, almond flour, eggs, Parmesan cheese, garlic powder, salt, and pepper. Mix until well combined.

2. Heat olive oil in a skillet over medium heat.

3. Scoop about 2 tablespoons of the mixture and flatten it slightly in the skillet to form fritters. Cook for 3-4 minutes on each side or until golden brown and crispy.

4. Transfer the fritters to a paper towel-lined plate to absorb excess oil. Repeat with the remaining mixture.

5. Serve warm as an appetizer or side dish.

Keto Carrot Soup

INGREDIENTS
- · - 2 cups chopped carrots
- · - 1 onion, diced
- · - 2 cloves garlic, minced
- · - 4 cups vegetable or chicken broth (960 ml)
- · - 1 cup heavy cream (240 ml)

- · - 1 tsp ground cumin
- · - Salt and pepper to taste
- · - Olive oil for sautéing
- · - Fresh herbs for garnish (optional)

DIRECTIONS

1. In a large pot, heat olive oil over medium heat. Add the diced onion and cook until softened, about 5 minutes.
2. Add the minced garlic and chopped carrots, cooking for an additional 5 minutes.
3. Pour in the broth, add ground cumin, and bring to a boil. Reduce heat and simmer for about 20 minutes or until the carrots are tender.
4. Remove from heat and use an immersion blender to puree the soup until smooth (or carefully transfer to a blender in batches).
5. Stir in the heavy cream, and season with salt and pepper to taste. Heat for a few more minutes if necessary.
6. Serve warm, garnished with fresh herbs if desired.

Roasted Beet Salad with Goat Cheese

INGREDIENTS

- · - 2 medium beets, peeled and diced
- · - 2 tbsp olive oil
- · - Salt and pepper to taste
- · - 2 cups mixed greens (e.g., spinach, arugula)
- · - 1/4 cup goat cheese, crumbled
- · - 1/4 cup walnuts, chopped (optional)
- · - Balsamic vinegar for drizzling

DIRECTIONS

1. Preheat the oven to 400°F (200°C). Line a baking sheet with parchment paper.
2. Toss the diced beets with olive oil, salt, and pepper, then spread them in a single layer on the baking sheet.
3. Roast for 25-30 minutes, or until tender, turning halfway through.
4. In a bowl, combine the mixed greens, roasted beets, goat cheese, and walnuts if using.
5. Drizzle with balsamic vinegar before serving. Enjoy this colorful salad warm or at room temperature!

Keto Beet Hummus

INGREDIENTS

- · - 1 cup cooked beets, diced
- · - 1/4 cup tahini
- · - 2 tbsp olive oil
- · - 2 tbsp lemon juice
- · - 1 garlic clove
- · - Salt and pepper to taste
- · - Water as needed for consistency

DIRECTIONS

1. In a food processor, combine the cooked beets, tahini, olive oil, lemon juice, garlic, salt, and pepper.
2. Blend until smooth, adding water a tablespoon at a time to reach your desired consistency.
3. Taste and adjust seasoning if necessary.
4. Serve the beet hummus with veggie sticks or as a spread on keto-friendly crackers.

Beet and Feta Cheese Egg Muffins

INGREDIENTS
- - 1 cup cooked beets, diced
- - 6 large eggs
- - 1/2 cup feta cheese, crumbled
- - 1/2 cup spinach, chopped
- - Salt and pepper to taste
- - Olive oil or cooking spray for greasing

DIRECTIONS

1. Preheat the oven to 350°F (175°C) and grease a muffin tin.
2. In a large bowl, whisk the eggs and season with salt and pepper.
3. Stir in the diced beets, feta cheese, and chopped spinach until well combined.
4. Pour the mixture evenly into the muffin tin, filling each cup about 3/4 full.
5. Bake for 20-25 minutes, or until the egg muffins are set and slightly golden.
6. Allow to cool for a few minutes before removing from the tin. Serve warm or store in the fridge for meal prep.

Keto Apple Crisp (using Chayote)

INGREDIENTS
- - 2 medium chayote squash, peeled and diced (a low-carb substitute for apples)
- - 1/4 cup almond flour
- - 1/4 cup coconut flour
- - 1/4 cup erythritol or your preferred keto sweetener
- - 1 tsp cinnamon
- - 1/4 cup unsalted butter, melted
- - 1/2 tsp vanilla extract
- - 1/4 cup chopped walnuts or pecans (optional)

DIRECTIONS

1. Preheat the oven to 350°F (175°C) and grease an 8x8-inch baking dish.
2. In a bowl, combine the diced chayote with 1 tablespoon of erythritol and cinnamon. Spread evenly in the baking dish.
3. In another bowl, mix almond flour, coconut flour, remaining erythritol, melted butter, and vanilla extract until crumbly. Stir in the chopped nuts if using.
4. Sprinkle the topping evenly over the chayote mixture.
5. Bake for 25-30 minutes or until the topping is golden brown. Allow to cool slightly before serving.

Keto "Apple" Salad with Celery and Walnuts

INGREDIENTS
- - 1 cup diced green bell pepper (to mimic the crunch of apples)
- - 1/2 cup celery, chopped
- - 1/4 cup walnuts, chopped
- - 1/4 cup mayonnaise (preferably sugar-free)
- - 1 tbsp apple cider vinegar
- - 1 tsp erythritol or your preferred keto sweetener
- - Salt and pepper to taste

DIRECTIONS

1. In a large bowl, combine the diced green bell pepper, chopped celery, and walnuts.
2. In a separate small bowl, whisk together the mayonnaise, apple cider vinegar, erythritol, salt, and pepper.

3. Pour the dressing over the vegetable mixture and stir until well combined.

4. Chill in the refrigerator for at least 30 minutes before serving.

Keto Cinnamon "Apple" Smoothie (using Zucchini)

INGREDIENTS
- · - 1 cup frozen zucchini, chopped (to replace apple texture)
- · - 1/2 cup unsweetened almond milk
- · - 1 tbsp almond butter
- · - 1 tbsp erythritol or your preferred sweetener
- · - 1 tsp cinnamon
- · - 1/2 tsp vanilla extract
- · - Ice cubes (optional)

DIRECTIONS

1. In a blender, combine the frozen zucchini, almond milk, almond butter, erythritol, cinnamon, vanilla extract, and ice cubes if desired.

2. Blend until smooth and creamy.

3. Taste and adjust sweetness or cinnamon to your liking. Pour into a glass and enjoy!

Keto Beef Stroganoff

INGREDIENTS
- · - 1 lb (450 g) beef sirloin or tenderloin, sliced into thin strips
- · - 2 tbsp olive oil
- · - 1 onion, diced
- · - 2 cloves garlic, minced
- · - 8 oz (225 g) mushrooms, sliced
- · - 1 cup beef broth (240 ml)
- · - 1/2 cup sour cream (120 ml)
- · - 1 tsp Worcestershire sauce (optional)
- · - Salt and pepper to taste
- · - Fresh parsley for garnish

DIRECTIONS

1. In a large skillet, heat the olive oil over medium-high heat. Add the sliced beef and cook until browned, about 3-4 minutes. Remove the beef from the skillet and set aside.

2. In the same skillet, add the diced onion and cook until softened, about 5 minutes. Add the minced garlic and mushrooms, cooking for another 5 minutes until the mushrooms are tender.

3. Pour in the beef broth and Worcestershire sauce, bringing it to a simmer. Let it cook for about 5 minutes.

4. Lower the heat and stir in the sour cream, mixing until well combined. Return the beef to the skillet and cook for an additional 2-3 minutes until heated through.

5. Season with salt and pepper to taste and garnish with fresh parsley before serving.

Keto Beef Tacos (using Lettuce Wraps)

INGREDIENTS
- · - 1 lb (450 g) ground beef
- · - 1 tbsp taco seasoning (homemade or store-bought, ensuring it's low-carb)
- · - 1/4 cup water
- · - Lettuce leaves (such as romaine or iceberg) for wrapping
- · - Toppings: diced tomatoes, shredded cheese, avocado, sour cream, cilantro, etc.

DIRECTIONS

1. In a skillet over medium heat, cook the ground beef until browned, breaking it apart with a spatula.
2. Drain any excess fat, then add the taco seasoning and water. Stir to combine and simmer for about 5 minutes until the sauce thickens.
3. To serve, spoon the beef mixture into lettuce leaves and add your favorite toppings. Enjoy as a low-carb taco!

Keto Beef and Broccoli Stir-Fry

INGREDIENTS

- · -1 lb (450 g) flank steak, thinly sliced
- · - 2 cups broccoli florets
- · - 2 tbsp soy sauce or coconut aminos
- · - 1 tbsp sesame oil
- · - 2 cloves garlic, minced
- · - 1 tbsp grated fresh ginger (optional)
- · - 1 tbsp olive oil
- · - Sesame seeds for garnish (optional)
- · - Green onions for garnish (optional)

DIRECTIONS

1. In a bowl, combine the sliced beef with soy sauce or coconut aminos, garlic, and ginger. Let it marinate for about 15 minutes.
2. In a large skillet or wok, heat the olive oil over medium-high heat. Add the marinated beef and stir-fry until browned, about 3-4 minutes. Remove the beef from the skillet and set aside.
3. In the same skillet, add the broccoli and a splash of water. Cover and steam for about 3-4 minutes until the broccoli is tender-crisp.
4. Return the beef to the skillet, drizzle with sesame oil, and stir to combine. Cook for an additional 2-3 minutes until heated through.
5. Garnish with sesame seeds and green onions before serving.

Cheesy Broccoli Casserole

INGREDIENTS

- · - 4 cups broccoli florets (fresh or frozen)
- · - 1 cup shredded cheddar cheese (about 120 g)
- · - 1/2 cup cream cheese (about 115 g), softened
- · - 1/2 cup heavy cream (120 ml)
- · - 1/2 tsp garlic powder
- · - 1/2 tsp onion powder
- · - Salt and pepper to taste
- · - 1/4 cup grated Parmesan cheese (optional)

DIRECTIONS

1. Preheat the oven to 350°F (175°C) and grease a baking dish.
2. Steam the broccoli florets until just tender, about 5-7 minutes. Drain and set aside.
3. In a large mixing bowl, combine the cheddar cheese, cream cheese, heavy cream, garlic powder, onion powder, salt, and pepper. Mix until smooth.
4. Fold the steamed broccoli into the cheese mixture until well coated.
5. Transfer the mixture to the prepared baking dish and sprinkle with grated Parmesan cheese if desired.
6. Bake for 25-30 minutes, or until bubbly and golden on top. Let cool slightly before serving.

Garlic Butter Broccoli

INGREDIENTS
- · - 4 cups broccoli florets
- · - 4 tbsp unsalted butter
- · - 3 cloves garlic, minced
- · - Salt and pepper to taste
- · - Lemon wedges for serving (optional)

DIRECTIONS

1. In a large pot of boiling salted water, blanch the broccoli florets for about 3-4 minutes until bright green and tender-crisp. Drain and set aside.

2. In a skillet, melt the butter over medium heat. Add the minced garlic and sauté for 1-2 minutes until fragrant.

3. Add the blanched broccoli to the skillet and toss to coat with the garlic butter. Season with salt and pepper to taste.

4. Cook for an additional 2-3 minutes until heated through. Serve with lemon wedges if desired.

Broccoli and Cheese Stuffed Chicken Breast

INGREDIENTS
- · - 2 large chicken breasts
- · - 1 cup broccoli florets, steamed and chopped
- · - 1/2 cup cream cheese (about 115 g), softened
- · - 1/2 cup shredded cheddar cheese (about 120 g)
- · - 1/2 tsp garlic powder
- · - Salt and pepper to taste
- · - Olive oil for drizzling

DIRECTIONS

1. Preheat the oven to 375°F (190°C) and grease a baking dish.

2. In a mixing bowl, combine the steamed and chopped broccoli, cream cheese, cheddar cheese, garlic powder, salt, and pepper. Mix until well combined.

3. Carefully slice a pocket into each chicken breast and stuff with the broccoli and cheese mixture.

4. Place the stuffed chicken breasts in the baking dish, drizzle with olive oil, and season with salt and pepper.

5. Bake for 25-30 minutes, or until the chicken is cooked through and reaches an internal temperature of 165°F (75°C). Let rest for a few minutes before serving.

Keto Chicken with Tomato Basil Sauce

INGREDIENTS
- · - 4 chicken breasts
- · - 2 tablespoons olive oil
- · - 1 can (14 oz) diced tomatoes (or 2 cups fresh tomatoes, diced)
- · - 3 cloves garlic (minced)
- · - 1 teaspoon dried basil (or 1 tablespoon fresh basil)
- · - Salt and pepper (to taste)
- · - 1/2 cup grated Parmesan cheese
- · - Fresh basil leaves (for garnish)

DIRECTIONS

1. **Cook the Chicken**: In a large skillet, heat olive oil over medium heat. Season chicken breasts with salt and pepper. Add to the skillet and cook for about 6-7 minutes on each side, until golden brown and cooked through. Remove from the skillet and set aside.

2. **Make the Sauce**: In the same skillet, add minced garlic and sauté for 1 minute. Add diced tomatoes and dried basil. Simmer for about 5-7 minutes until the sauce thickens slightly. Season with salt and pepper.

3. **Combine**: Return the chicken to the skillet, spooning the sauce over the top. Sprinkle with Parmesan cheese and cover the skillet. Cook for an additional 2-3 minutes until the cheese is melted.

4. **Serve**: Garnish with fresh basil leaves and serve.

Creamy Tomato Chicken Skillet

INGREDIENTS

- ·   - 4 chicken thighs (boneless, skinless)
- ·   - 2 tablespoons olive oil
- ·   - 1 can (14 oz) crushed tomatoes
- ·   - 1/2 cup heavy cream
- ·   - 2 cloves garlic (minced)
- ·   - 1 teaspoon Italian seasoning
- ·   - Salt and pepper (to taste)
- ·   - Fresh parsley (for garnish)

DIRECTIONS

1. **Cook the Chicken**: Heat olive oil in a large skillet over medium heat. Season chicken thighs with salt and pepper. Add to the skillet and cook for about 6-7 minutes on each side until golden brown. Remove and set aside.

2. **Make the Sauce**: In the same skillet, add minced garlic and sauté for 1 minute. Stir in crushed tomatoes, heavy cream, Italian seasoning, salt, and pepper. Simmer for about 5 minutes.

3. **Combine**: Return the chicken to the skillet and cook for an additional 5-7 minutes, or until the chicken is cooked through and the sauce has thickened.

4. **Serve**: Garnish with fresh parsley before serving.

Keto Chicken Caprese

INGREDIENTS

- ·   4 chicken breasts
- ·   - 2 tablespoons olive oil
- ·   - 1 cup cherry tomatoes (halved)
- ·   - 1 cup mozzarella cheese (shredded or sliced)
- ·   - 1/4 cup fresh basil (chopped)
- ·   - Balsamic glaze (for drizzling)
- ·   - Salt and pepper (to taste)

DIRECTIONS

1. **Cook the Chicken**: Preheat the oven to 400°F (200°C). In a skillet, heat olive oil over medium heat. Season chicken breasts with salt and pepper. Sear the chicken for about 5 minutes on each side until golden.

2. **Top with Tomatoes and Cheese**: Transfer the chicken to a baking dish. Top with cherry tomatoes and mozzarella cheese.

3. **Bake**: Bake in the preheated oven for 15-20 minutes until the chicken is cooked through and the cheese is melted.

4. **Serve**: Garnish with fresh basil and drizzle with balsamic glaze before serving.

Keto Chicken and Tomato Skewers

INGREDIENTS
- · - 1 pound chicken breast (cut into cubes)
- · - 1 cup cherry tomatoes
- · - 2 tablespoons olive oil
- · - 1 tablespoon Italian seasoning
- · - Salt and pepper (to taste)
- · - Fresh basil (for garnish)

DIRECTIONS

1. **Marinate the Chicken**: In a bowl, combine chicken cubes, olive oil, Italian seasoning, salt, and pepper. Mix well and let marinate for 15-30 minutes.

2. **Assemble the Skewers**: Thread chicken and cherry tomatoes alternately onto skewers.

3. **Grill**: Preheat the grill to medium heat. Grill the skewers for about 10-12 minutes, turning occasionally, until the chicken is cooked through.

4. **Serve**: Garnish with fresh basil and serve.

Keto Breakfast Casserole

INGREDIENTS
- · - 6 eggs
- · - 1 cup heavy cream
- · - 1 cup shredded cheese (cheddar or mozzarella)
- · - 1 cup diced cooked bacon or sausage
- · - 1 cup spinach (chopped)
- · - Salt and pepper (to taste)

DIRECTIONS

1. Preheat the oven to 350°F (175°C).

2. In a bowl, whisk together eggs, heavy cream, salt, and pepper.

3. Stir in cheese, bacon or sausage, and spinach.

4. Pour the mixture into a greased baking dish and bake for 30-35 minutes or until set. Cut into squares and serve.

Keto Chicken Salad

INGREDIENTS
- · - 2 cups cooked chicken (shredded)
- · - 1/2 cup mayonnaise
- · - 1 tablespoon Dijon mustard
- · - 1/4 cup celery (diced)
- · - 1/4 cup red onion (diced)
- · - Salt and pepper (to taste)
- · - Lettuce leaves (for serving)

DIRECTIONS

1. In a bowl, combine shredded chicken, mayonnaise, Dijon mustard, celery, red onion, salt, and pepper.

2. Mix until well combined. Serve on lettuce leaves or in avocado halves.

Zucchini Noodles with Pesto and Shrimp

INGREDIENTS

- · -2 medium zucchinis (spiralized)
- · - 1 pound shrimp (peeled and deveined)
- · - 2 tablespoons olive oil
- · - 1/4 cup pesto
- · - Salt and pepper (to taste)
- · - Parmesan cheese (for garnish)

DIRECTIONS

1. In a skillet, heat olive oil over medium heat. Add shrimp, seasoning with salt and pepper. Cook for 3-4 minutes until pink.
2. Add zucchini noodles to the skillet and toss with shrimp and pesto. Cook for an additional 2-3 minutes.
3. Serve garnished with Parmesan cheese.

Keto Beef Stir-Fry

INGREDIENTS

- · - 1 pound beef (sliced thin)
- · - 2 tablespoons soy sauce (or coconut aminos)
- · - 1 tablespoon sesame oil
- · - 1 cup bell peppers (sliced)
- · - 1 cup broccoli florets
- · - 2 cloves garlic (minced)
- · - Salt and pepper (to taste)

DIRECTIONS

. In a skillet, heat sesame oil over medium-high heat. Add sliced beef and cook until browned.
2. Add bell peppers, broccoli, garlic, soy sauce, salt, and pepper. Stir-fry for 5-7 minutes until veggies are tender.
3. Serve hot.

Keto Cauliflower Pizza

INGREDIENTS

- · - 1 head cauliflower (riced)
- · - 1 cup shredded mozzarella cheese
- · - 1/2 cup grated Parmesan cheese
- · - 2 eggs
- · - 1 teaspoon Italian seasoning
- · - Toppings of choice (pepperoni, bell peppers, olives, etc.)

DIRECTIONS

1. Preheat the oven to 425°F (220°C).
2. In a bowl, combine riced cauliflower, mozzarella, Parmesan, eggs, Italian seasoning, and mix well.
3. Spread the mixture onto a baking sheet to form a crust. Bake for 15-20 minutes until golden.
4. Remove from the oven, add toppings, and bake for an additional 10 minutes.

Keto Egg Muffins

INGREDIENTS

- · - 6 eggs
- · - 1/2 cup diced bell peppers
- · - 1/2 cup diced cooked sausage or ham
- · - 1/2 cup shredded cheese
- · - Salt and pepper (to taste)

DIRECTIONS

1. Preheat the oven to 350°F (175°C) and grease a muffin tin.
2. In a bowl, whisk eggs, then stir in bell peppers, sausage, cheese, salt, and pepper.
3. Pour the mixture into the muffin tin and bake for 18-20 minutes until set.

Keto Skillet Chicken Alfredo

INGREDIENTS

- · - 4 boneless, skinless chicken breasts
- · - 2 tablespoons olive oil
- · - 2 cups heavy cream
- · - 1 cup grated Parmesan cheese
- · - 2 cloves garlic (minced)
- · - Salt and pepper (to taste)
- · - Fresh parsley (for garnish)

DIRECTIONS

1. Heat olive oil in a large skillet over medium heat. Season chicken breasts with salt and pepper and cook for about 6-7 minutes on each side until cooked through. Remove from the skillet and set aside.
2. In the same skillet, add minced garlic and sauté for 1 minute. Pour in heavy cream and bring to a simmer.
3. Stir in Parmesan cheese and cook until the sauce thickens. Season with salt and pepper to taste.
4. Return the chicken to the skillet, coating it with the sauce. Garnish with chopped parsley before serving.

Keto Chicken Thighs with Creamy Mushroom Sauce

INGREDIENTS

- · - 4 chicken thighs (skin-on)
- · - 2 cups mushrooms (sliced)
- · - 1 cup heavy cream
- · - 2 tablespoons olive oil
- · - Salt and pepper (to taste)
- · - Fresh parsley (for garnish)

DIRECTIONS

1. In a skillet, heat olive oil over medium heat. Season chicken thighs with salt and pepper, and cook for 7-8 minutes on each side until cooked through. Remove and set aside.
2. In the same skillet, add mushrooms and cook until softened. Stir in heavy cream, salt, and pepper. Simmer for a few minutes until thickened.
3. Return chicken to the skillet, coating with the sauce. Garnish with parsley before serving.

Keto Shrimp and Broccoli Stir-Fry

INGREDIENTS
- · - 1 pound shrimp (peeled and deveined)
- · - 2 cups broccoli florets
- · - 2 tablespoons olive oil
- · - 2 cloves garlic (minced)
- · - 1 tablespoon soy sauce (or coconut aminos)
- · - Salt and pepper (to taste)
- · - Sesame seeds (for garnish)

DIRECTIONS

1. In a skillet, heat olive oil over medium-high heat. Add minced garlic and sauté for 30 seconds.

2. Add shrimp and cook until pink, about 3-4 minutes. Remove from skillet and set aside.

3. In the same skillet, add broccoli and a splash of water. Cover and steam for about 3-4 minutes until tender.

4. Add shrimp back to the skillet, pour in soy sauce, and stir to combine. Cook for an additional minute and season with salt and pepper. Garnish with sesame seeds before serving.

Keto Zucchini Noodles with Pesto and Chicken

INGREDIENTS
- · - 2 medium zucchinis (spiralized into noodles)
- · - 2 cooked chicken breasts (sliced)
- · - 1/4 cup pesto
- · - 1 tablespoon olive oil
- · - Salt and pepper (to taste)
- · - Grated Parmesan cheese (for serving)

DIRECTIONS

1. Heat olive oil in a skillet over medium heat. Add zucchini noodles and cook for 2-3 minutes until slightly tender.

2. Add sliced chicken and pesto to the skillet, stirring to combine. Cook for an additional 2-3 minutes until heated through.

3. Season with salt and pepper and serve topped with grated Parmesan cheese.

Cottage Cheese Pancakes

INGREDIENTS
- · - 1 cup cottage cheese
- · - 2 large eggs
- · - 1/4 cup almond flour
- · - 1 tsp baking powder
- · - Pinch of salt
- · - Butter or oil for cooking

DIRECTIONS

1. In a blender, combine cottage cheese, eggs, almond flour, baking powder, and salt. Blend until smooth.

2. Heat a non-stick skillet over medium heat and add a little butter or oil.

3. Pour batter into the skillet to form pancakes. Cook for about 2-3 minutes on each side, until golden brown.

4. Serve warm with sugar-free syrup or fresh berries.

Cottage Cheese and Spinach Bake

INGREDIENTS

- · - 2 cups cottage cheese
- · - 1 cup shredded mozzarella cheese
- · - 2 large eggs
- · - 1 cup spinach (fresh or frozen, thawed and drained)
- · - 1/2 tsp garlic powder
- · - Salt and pepper to taste
- · - Olive oil for greasing

DIRECTIONS

1. Preheat the oven to 350°F (175°C). Grease a baking dish with olive oil.
2. In a mixing bowl, combine cottage cheese, mozzarella cheese, eggs, spinach, garlic powder, salt, and pepper.
3. Pour the mixture into the prepared baking dish and spread evenly.
4. Bake for 30-35 minutes, until the top is golden and the center is set.
5. Allow to cool slightly before slicing and serving.

Savory Cottage Cheese Bowl

INGREDIENTS

- · - 1 cup cottage cheese
- · - 1/2 cucumber, diced
- · - 1/2 cup cherry tomatoes, halved
- · - 1/4 cup black olives, sliced
- · - Fresh herbs (dill or parsley), chopped
- · - 1 tbsp olive oil
- · - Salt and pepper to taste

DIRECTIONS

1. In a bowl, combine cottage cheese, cucumber, cherry tomatoes, olives, and herbs.
2. Drizzle with olive oil and season with salt and pepper.
3. Toss gently to combine and serve immediately.

Cottage Cheese Smoothie

INGREDIENTS

- · - 1/2 cup cottage cheese
- · - 1 cup unsweetened almond milk
- · - 1/2 avocado
- · - Handful of spinach
- · - Ice cubes (optional)
- · - Sweetener (optional, to taste)

DIRECTIONS

1. In a blender, combine cottage cheese, almond milk, avocado, spinach, and ice cubes.
2. Blend until smooth and creamy.
3. Taste and adjust sweetness if desired. Serve chilled.

Cottage Cheese Omelette

INGREDIENTS
- - 3 large eggs
- - 1 cup cottage cheese
- - 1/2 bell pepper, diced
- - 1/4 onion, diced
- - Salt and pepper to taste
- - Butter or oil for cooking

DIRECTIONS

1. In a bowl, whisk together eggs, salt, and pepper.
2. In a skillet, heat butter or oil over medium heat. Add bell pepper and onion, cooking until softened.
3. Pour the egg mixture over the vegetables. Cook until the edges start to set.
4. Spoon cottage cheese onto one half of the omelette. Carefully fold the other half over and cook for another minute until the eggs are fully set.
5. Slide onto a plate and serve warm.

Keto Almond Flour Pancakes

INGREDIENTS
- - 1 cup almond flour
- - 2 large eggs
- - 1/4 cup unsweetened almond milk
- - 1 tsp baking powder
- - 1 tsp vanilla extract
- - Pinch of salt
- - Butter (for cooking)

DIRECTIONS

1. In a bowl, mix almond flour, baking powder, and salt.
2. In another bowl, whisk together eggs, almond milk, and vanilla extract.
3. Combine the wet and dry ingredients, mixing until smooth.
4. Heat a skillet over medium heat and add butter.
5. Pour batter into the skillet to form pancakes. Cook until bubbles form, then flip and cook until golden brown.
6. Serve with sugar-free syrup or berries.

Keto Coconut Flour Bread

INGREDIENTS
- - 1/2 cup coconut flour
- - 6 large eggs
- - 1/4 cup melted butter or coconut oil
- - 1/2 tsp baking soda
- - 1/2 tsp salt
- - 1/4 cup unsweetened almond milk

DIRECTIONS

1. Preheat the oven to 350°F (175°C). Grease a loaf pan.
2. In a bowl, combine coconut flour, baking soda, and salt.
3. In another bowl, whisk eggs, melted butter, and almond milk.
4. Mix the wet ingredients into the dry ingredients until well combined.
5. Pour the batter into the prepared loaf pan and smooth the top.
6. Bake for 30-35 minutes until a toothpick comes out clean. Let cool before slicing.

Keto Cauliflower Pizza Crust

INGREDIENTS

- · - 1 medium cauliflower, riced (about 2 cups)
- · - 1 cup shredded mozzarella cheese
- · - 1/2 cup almond flour
- · - 2 large eggs
- · - 1 tsp Italian seasoning
- · - Salt and pepper to taste

DIRECTIONS

1. Preheat the oven to 400°F (200°C). Line a baking sheet with parchment paper.

2. Steam or microwave the riced cauliflower until tender, then drain excess moisture.

3. In a bowl, combine cauliflower, mozzarella cheese, almond flour, eggs, Italian seasoning, salt, and pepper.

4. Spread the mixture onto the baking sheet, forming a pizza crust.

5. Bake for 20-25 minutes until golden.

6. Add your favorite toppings and bake again until cheese is melted.

Keto Chocolate Chip Cookies

INGREDIENTS

- · - 1 cup almond flour
- · - 1/4 cup coconut flour
- · - 1/2 tsp baking soda
- · - 1/4 cup butter, softened
- · - 1/4 cup erythritol or your preferred sweetener
- · - 1 large egg
- · - 1/2 tsp vanilla extract
- · - 1/2 cup sugar-free chocolate chips

DIRECTIONS

1. Preheat the oven to 350°F (175°C). Line a baking sheet with parchment paper.

2. In a bowl, mix almond flour, coconut flour, and baking soda.

3. In another bowl, cream together butter and erythritol. Add egg and vanilla, mixing until smooth.

4. Combine wet and dry ingredients, then fold in chocolate chips.

5. Scoop dough onto the baking sheet, spacing them apart.

6. Bake for 10-12 minutes until edges are golden. Let cool before serving.

Keto Breaded Chicken Tenders

INGREDIENTS

- · - 1 lb chicken tenders
- · - 1/2 cup almond flour
- · - 1/4 cup grated Parmesan cheese
- · - 1 tsp garlic powder
- · - 1 tsp paprika
- · - Salt and pepper to taste
- · - 2 large eggs (beaten)
- · - Olive oil for frying

DIRECTIONS

1. In a bowl, mix almond flour, Parmesan cheese, garlic powder, paprika, salt, and pepper.

2. Dip each chicken tender in the beaten eggs, then coat with the almond flour mixture.

3. Heat olive oil in a skillet over medium heat.

4. Cook chicken tenders for 5-7 minutes on each side until golden brown and cooked through.
5. Serve with your favorite dipping sauce.

Keto Chicken Cutlets

INGREDIENTS
- - 1 lb chicken breast, pounded thin
- - 1/2 cup almond flour
- - 1/4 cup grated Parmesan cheese
- - 1 tsp garlic powder
- - 1 tsp paprika
- - Salt and pepper to taste
- - 2 large eggs (beaten)
- - Olive oil or butter for frying

DIRECTIONS
1. In a bowl, mix almond flour, Parmesan cheese, garlic powder, paprika, salt, and pepper.
2. Dip each chicken cutlet in the beaten eggs, then coat with the almond flour mixture.
3. Heat olive oil or butter in a skillet over medium heat.
4. Cook the chicken cutlets for about 5-7 minutes on each side until golden brown and cooked through.
5. Serve with a side salad or your favorite keto dipping sauce.

Keto Zucchini Cutlets

INGREDIENTS
- - 2 medium zucchinis, grated
- - 1/2 cup almond flour
- - 1/4 cup grated Parmesan cheese
- - 1 large egg
- - 1 tsp garlic powder
- - Salt and pepper to taste
- - Olive oil for frying

DIRECTIONS
1. Squeeze out excess moisture from grated zucchini using a clean kitchen towel.
2. In a bowl, combine zucchini, almond flour, Parmesan cheese, egg, garlic powder, salt, and pepper.
3. Heat olive oil in a skillet over medium heat.
4. Form small patties from the zucchini mixture and place them in the skillet.
5. Cook for about 4-5 minutes on each side until golden brown.
6. Serve with a dollop of sour cream or Greek yogurt.

Keto Cauliflower Cutlets

INGREDIENTS
- - 2 cups cauliflower rice (fresh or frozen)
- - 1/2 cup almond flour
- - 1/4 cup grated cheese (like cheddar or mozzarella)
- - 1 large egg
- - 1 tsp Italian seasoning
- - Salt and pepper to taste
- - Olive oil for frying

DIRECTIONS
1. Steam or microwave cauliflower rice until tender, then drain excess moisture.
2. In a bowl, combine cauliflower rice, almond flour, cheese, egg, Italian seasoning, salt, and pepper.
3. Heat olive oil in a skillet over medium heat.
4. Form the mixture into cutlets and place them in the skillet.
5. Cook for 4-5 minutes on each side until golden brown and crispy.
6. Serve with marinara sauce or a side salad.

Keto Eggplant Cutlets

INGREDIENTS
- · - 1 medium eggplant, sliced into 1/4-inch rounds
- · - 1/2 cup almond flour
- · - 1/4 cup grated Parmesan cheese
- · - 1 tsp Italian seasoning
- · - Salt and pepper to taste
- · - 2 large eggs (beaten)
- · - Olive oil for frying

DIRECTIONS
1. Sprinkle salt on eggplant slices and let them sit for 30 minutes to draw out moisture. Rinse and pat dry.
2. In a bowl, mix almond flour, Parmesan cheese, Italian seasoning, salt, and pepper.
3. Dip eggplant slices in the beaten eggs, then coat with the almond flour mixture.
4. Heat olive oil in a skillet over medium heat.
5. Fry eggplant cutlets for about 4-5 minutes on each side until golden brown.
6. Serve with a marinara sauce or a fresh salad.

Keto Salmon Cutlets

INGREDIENTS
- · - 1 can (14 oz) salmon, drained and flaked (or cooked salmon)
- · - 1/2 cup almond flour
- · - 1/4 cup grated Parmesan cheese
- · - 1 large egg
- · - 1 tbsp Dijon mustard
- · - 1 tsp lemon juice
- · - Salt and pepper to taste
- · - Olive oil for frying

DIRECTIONS
1. In a bowl, combine flaked salmon, almond flour, Parmesan cheese, egg, mustard, lemon juice, salt, and pepper.
2. Form the mixture into cutlets.
3. Heat olive oil in a skillet over medium heat.
4. Fry salmon cutlets for about 3-4 minutes on each side until golden brown.
5. Serve with a side of tartar sauce or a fresh garden salad.

Keto Zucchini Fritters

INGREDIENTS
- · - 2 medium zucchinis, grated
- · - 1/2 cup almond flour
- · - 1/4 cup grated Parmesan cheese
- · - 1 large egg
- · - 2 green onions, chopped
- · - 1 tsp garlic powder
- · - Salt and pepper to taste
- · - Olive oil for frying

DIRECTIONS

1. Squeeze excess moisture from the grated zucchini using a clean kitchen towel.
2. In a bowl, combine zucchini, almond flour, Parmesan cheese, egg, green onions, garlic powder, salt, and pepper.
3. Heat olive oil in a skillet over medium heat.
4. Drop spoonfuls of the mixture into the skillet and flatten slightly to form fritters.
5. Cook for about 4-5 minutes on each side until golden brown and crispy.
6. Serve warm with sour cream or Greek yogurt.

Keto Cauliflower Fritters

INGREDIENTS
- · - 2 cups cauliflower rice (fresh or frozen)
- · - 1/2 cup almond flour
- · - 1/4 cup shredded cheese (like cheddar or mozzarella)
- · - 1 large egg
- · - 1 tsp Italian seasoning
- · - Salt and pepper to taste
- · - Olive oil for frying

DIRECTIONS

1. Steam or microwave the cauliflower rice until tender, then drain any excess moisture.
2. In a bowl, mix cauliflower rice, almond flour, cheese, egg, Italian seasoning, salt, and pepper until well combined.
3. Heat olive oil in a skillet over medium heat.
4. Form the mixture into small fritters and place them in the skillet.
5. Cook for 4-5 minutes on each side until golden brown and crispy.
6. Serve with marinara sauce or a dipping sauce of your choice.

Keto Spinach and Feta Fritters

INGREDIENTS
- · - 2 cups fresh spinach, chopped (or 1 cup frozen, thawed and drained)
- · - 1/2 cup almond flour
- · - 1/4 cup crumbled feta cheese
- · - 1 large egg
- · - 1/4 cup diced onion
- · - 1 tsp garlic powder
- · - Salt and pepper to taste
- · - Olive oil for frying

DIRECTIONS

1. If using fresh spinach, sauté it in a pan until wilted. Let it cool and then squeeze out excess moisture.
2. In a bowl, combine spinach, almond flour, feta cheese, egg, onion, garlic powder, salt, and pepper.
3. Heat olive oil in a skillet over medium heat.
4. Drop spoonfuls of the mixture into the skillet and flatten them slightly.
5. Cook for about 4-5 minutes on each side until golden brown.
6. Serve with tzatziki sauce or sour cream.

Keto Broccoli Fritters

INGREDIENTS

- - 2 cups broccoli florets, steamed and finely chopped
- - 1/2 cup almond flour
- - 1/4 cup grated Parmesan cheese
- - 1 large egg
- - 1/4 tsp red pepper flakes (optional)
- - Salt and pepper to taste
- - Olive oil for frying

DIRECTIONS

1. In a bowl, combine chopped broccoli, almond flour, Parmesan cheese, egg, red pepper flakes, salt, and pepper.
2. Heat olive oil in a skillet over medium heat.
3. Form the mixture into fritters and place them in the skillet.
4. Cook for 4-5 minutes on each side until golden brown.
5. Serve warm with a dipping sauce of your choice.

Keto Cheese and Jalapeño Fritters

INGREDIENTS

- - 1 cup shredded cheese (cheddar or mozzarella)
- - 1/2 cup almond flour
- - 1 large egg
- - 1/4 cup diced jalapeños (fresh or pickled)
- - 1 tsp garlic powder
- - Salt and pepper to taste
- - Olive oil for frying

DIRECTIONS

1. In a bowl, combine shredded cheese, almond flour, egg, jalapeños, garlic powder, salt, and pepper.
2. Heat olive oil in a skillet over medium heat.
3. Drop spoonfuls of the mixture into the skillet, flattening them slightly.
4. Cook for about 3-4 minutes on each side until golden brown and crispy.
5. Serve warm with salsa or guacamole.

Keto Zucchini Noodles (Zoodles)

INGREDIENTS
- · - 2 medium zucchinis
- · - 2 tbsp olive oil
- · - 2 cloves garlic, minced
- · - Salt and pepper to taste
- · - Grated Parmesan cheese (optional)

DIRECTIONS

1. Using a spiralizer or a vegetable peeler, create zucchini noodles from the zucchinis.

2. In a skillet, heat olive oil over medium heat. Add minced garlic and sauté for about 30 seconds.

3. Add the zucchini noodles to the skillet and cook for 3-4 minutes until just tender. Season with salt and pepper.

4. Serve immediately, topped with grated Parmesan cheese if desired.

Keto Zucchini Fritters

INGREDIENTS
- · - 2 medium zucchinis, grated
- · - 1/2 cup almond flour
- · - 1/4 cup grated Parmesan cheese
- · - 1 large egg
- · - 2 green onions, chopped
- · - 1 tsp garlic powder
- · - Salt and pepper to taste
- · - Olive oil for frying

DIRECTIONS

1. Squeeze excess moisture from grated zucchini using a clean kitchen towel.

2. In a bowl, combine zucchini, almond flour, Parmesan cheese, egg, green onions, garlic powder, salt, and pepper.

3. Heat olive oil in a skillet over medium heat. Drop spoonfuls of the mixture into the skillet and flatten slightly.

4. Cook for about 4-5 minutes on each side until golden brown and crispy.

5. Serve warm with sour cream or Greek yogurt

Keto Stuffed Zucchini Boats

INGREDIENTS
- · - 2 medium zucchinis, halved lengthwise
- · - 1 cup ground meat (beef, turkey, or chicken)
- · - 1/2 cup diced tomatoes (canned or fresh)
- · - 1/4 cup grated cheese (like mozzarella or cheddar)
- · - 1 tsp Italian seasoning
- · - Salt and pepper to taste
- · - Olive oil for drizzling

DIRECTIONS

1. Preheat the oven to 375°F (190°C). Scoop out the center of the zucchini halves to create boats.

2. In a skillet, brown the ground meat over medium heat. Add diced tomatoes, Italian seasoning, salt, and pepper. Cook for about 5 minutes.

3. Place the zucchini boats on a baking sheet. Fill each boat with the meat mixture and top with grated cheese.

4. Drizzle with olive oil and bake for 20-25 minutes until the zucchini is tender and the cheese is melted.
5. Serve warm.

Keto Zucchini Casserole

INGREDIENTS
- · - 2 medium zucchinis, sliced
- · - 1 cup shredded cheese (like cheddar)
- · - 1/2 cup heavy cream
- · - 1/2 cup grated Parmesan cheese
- · - 2 large eggs
- · - 1 tsp garlic powder
- · - Salt and pepper to taste

DIRECTIONS
1. Preheat the oven to 350°F (175°C). Grease a baking dish.
2. In a bowl, whisk together heavy cream, eggs, garlic powder, salt, and pepper.
3. Layer zucchini slices in the greased baking dish. Pour the cream mixture over the zucchini and sprinkle with shredded cheese and Parmesan cheese.
4. Bake for 30-35 minutes until the casserole is set and golden on top.
5. Let cool slightly before serving.

Keto Zucchini Chips

INGREDIENTS
- · - 2 medium zucchinis, thinly sliced
- · - 2 tbsp olive oil
- · - 1 tsp garlic powder
- · - 1 tsp paprika
- · - Salt and pepper to taste

DIRECTIONS
1. Preheat the oven to 225°F (110°C). Line a baking sheet with parchment paper.
2. In a bowl, toss zucchini slices with olive oil, garlic powder, paprika, salt, and pepper.
3. Arrange the zucchini slices in a single layer on the prepared baking sheet.
4. Bake for 2-3 hours, flipping halfway through, until the chips are crispy.
5. Allow to cool and serve as a crunchy snack.

Roasted Beet Salad

INGREDIENTS
- · - 2 medium beets, peeled and diced
- · - 2 cups mixed greens (spinach, arugula, or baby kale)
- · - 1/4 cup crumbled feta cheese
- · - 1/4 cup walnuts, chopped
- · - 2 tbsp olive oil
- · - 1 tbsp balsamic vinegar
- · - Salt and pepper to taste

DIRECTIONS
1. Preheat the oven to 400°F (200°C). Toss the diced beets with olive oil, salt, and pepper.
2. Spread the beets on a baking sheet and roast for 30-35 minutes until tender.
3. In a bowl, combine mixed greens, roasted beets, feta cheese, and walnuts.

4. Drizzle with balsamic vinegar and toss gently before serving.

Keto Beet Hummus

INGREDIENTS
- · - 1 cup cooked beets, diced
- · - 1/4 cup tahini
- · - 2 tbsp olive oil
- · - 1 garlic clove, minced
- · - 1 tbsp lemon juice
- · - Salt and pepper to taste

DIRECTIONS
1. In a food processor, combine cooked beets, tahini, olive oil, garlic, lemon juice, salt, and pepper.
2. Blend until smooth, adding a little water if needed to reach desired consistency.
3. Serve as a dip with veggie sticks or spread on low-carb crackers.

Keto Beet and Goat Cheese Salad

INGREDIENTS
- · - 2 medium beets, roasted and sliced
- · - 4 cups arugula or mixed greens
- · - 1/4 cup goat cheese, crumbled
- · - 1/4 cup pecans, toasted
- · - 2 tbsp olive oil
- · - 1 tbsp apple cider vinegar
- · - Salt and pepper to taste

DIRECTIONS
1. Roast beets at 400°F (200°C) for 30-35 minutes until tender. Let cool, peel, and slice.
2. In a large bowl, combine arugula, sliced beets, goat cheese, and toasted pecans.
3. Drizzle with olive oil and apple cider vinegar, then season with salt and pepper. Toss gently before serving.

Keto Beet Soup (Borscht)

INGREDIENTS
- · - 2 medium beets, peeled and grated
- · - 1 small onion, chopped
- · - 1 garlic clove, minced
- · - 4 cups vegetable or chicken broth
- · - 1/2 cup sour cream (for serving)
- · - 2 tbsp olive oil
- · - Salt and pepper to taste
- · - Fresh dill (optional, for garnish)

DIRECTIONS
. In a pot, heat olive oil over medium heat. Add onion and garlic, sautéing until soft.
2. Add grated beets and broth to the pot. Bring to a boil, then reduce heat and simmer for 20-25 minutes until beets are tender.
3. Season with salt and pepper. Use an immersion blender to puree the soup until smooth, or leave it chunky if desired.
4. Serve hot, topped with a dollop of sour cream and fresh dill if desired.

Keto Beet and Avocado Salad

INGREDIENTS

- · - 1 cup cooked beets, diced
- · - 1 ripe avocado, diced
- · - 2 cups mixed greens
- · - 1/4 cup walnuts, chopped
- · - 2 tbsp olive oil
- · - 1 tbsp lemon juice
- · - Salt and pepper to taste

DIRECTIONS

1. In a large bowl, combine mixed greens, diced beets, avocado, and walnuts.

2. Drizzle with olive oil and lemon juice, then season with salt and pepper.

3. Toss gently and serve immediately.

Keto Pumpkin Soup

INGREDIENTS

- · - 1 can (15 oz) pumpkin puree (unsweetened)
- · - 2 cups vegetable or chicken broth
- · - 1/2 cup heavy cream
- · - 1 onion, chopped
- · - 2 cloves garlic, minced
- · - 1 tsp pumpkin pie spice
- · - 2 tbsp olive oil
- · - Salt and pepper to taste
- · - Fresh parsley (for garnish)

DIRECTIONS

1. In a pot, heat olive oil over medium heat. Add onion and garlic, sautéing until soft.

2. Stir in pumpkin puree, broth, and pumpkin pie spice. Bring to a simmer.

3. Reduce heat and stir in heavy cream. Season with salt and pepper to taste.

4. Use an immersion blender to blend until smooth, or transfer to a blender in batches.

5. Serve hot, garnished with fresh parsley.

Keto Pumpkin Muffins

INGREDIENTS

- · - 1 cup almond flour
- · - 1/2 cup pumpkin puree (unsweetened)
- · - 3 large eggs
- · - 1/4 cup erythritol or your preferred sweetener
- · - 1 tsp baking powder
- · - 1/2 tsp baking soda
- · - 1 tsp pumpkin pie spice
- · - 1/4 cup melted coconut oil or butter,1/2 tsp vanilla extract

DIRECTIONS

1. Preheat the oven to 350°F (175°C). Line a muffin tin with paper liners.

2. In a bowl, mix almond flour, erythritol, baking powder, baking soda, and pumpkin pie spice.

3. In another bowl, combine pumpkin puree, eggs, melted coconut oil, and vanilla extract.

4. Mix wet ingredients into dry ingredients until well combined.

5. Divide the batter among the muffin cups.

6. Bake for 20-25 minutes or until a toothpick comes out clean. Let cool before serving.

Keto Pumpkin Bread

INGREDIENTS
- · - 1 1/2 cups almond flour
- · - 1/2 cup pumpkin puree (unsweetened)
- · - 3 large eggs
- · - 1/4 cup erythritol or your preferred sweetener
- · - 1/4 cup coconut oil or melted butter
- · - 1 tsp baking powder
- · - 1 tsp pumpkin pie spice,1/2 tsp cinnamon,1/4 tsp salt

DIRECTIONS

1. Preheat the oven to 350°F (175°C). Grease a loaf pan.
2. In a bowl, mix almond flour, erythritol, baking powder, pumpkin pie spice, cinnamon, and salt.
3. In another bowl, combine pumpkin puree, eggs, and melted coconut oil.
4. Mix the wet ingredients into the dry ingredients until well combined.
5. Pour the batter into the prepared loaf pan and smooth the top.
6. Bake for 30-35 minutes or until a toothpick comes out clean. Let cool before slicing.

Keto Pumpkin Spice Latte

INGREDIENTS
- · - 1 cup brewed coffee
- · - 1/2 cup unsweetened almond milk (or coconut milk)
- · - 2 tbsp pumpkin puree (unsweetened)
- · - 1 tbsp erythritol or your preferred sweetener
- · - 1/2 tsp pumpkin pie spice
- · - 1/2 tsp vanilla extract
- · - Whipped cream (optional, for topping)

DIRECTIONS

1. In a small saucepan, combine almond milk, pumpkin puree, erythritol, pumpkin pie spice, and vanilla extract. Heat over medium until warm.
2. Whisk until well combined and frothy.
3. Pour brewed coffee into a mug and top with the pumpkin mixture.
4. Add whipped cream if desired and sprinkle with more pumpkin pie spice. Serve warm.

Keto Pumpkin Cheesecake Bars

INGREDIENTS
- · - **For the crust**:
- · - 1 1/2 cups almond flour
- · - 1/4 cup melted butter,- 2 tbsp erythritol, - 1/2 tsp cinnamon,For the filling**:
- · - 16 oz cream cheese, softened
- · - 1 cup pumpkin puree (unsweetened)
- · - 3 large eggs,1/2 cup erythritol,1 tsp vanilla extract
- · - 1 tsp pumpkin pie spice

DIRECTIONS

1. Preheat the oven to 350°F (175°C). Grease a baking dish.
2. In a bowl, mix almond flour, melted butter, erythritol, and cinnamon to form the crust. Press into the bottom of the baking dish.
3. Bake the crust for 10-12 minutes until lightly golden.
4. In another bowl, beat cream cheese until smooth. Add pumpkin puree, eggs, erythritol, vanilla extract, and pumpkin pie spice. Mix until well combined.

5. Pour the filling over the baked crust and spread evenly.

6. Bake for 25-30 minutes until set. Let cool, then refrigerate before slicing into bars.

Keto Cucumber Salad

INGREDIENTS

- · - 2 large cucumbers, thinly sliced
- · - 1/4 red onion, thinly sliced
- · - 1/4 cup chopped fresh dill
- · - 1/2 cup sour cream or Greek yogurt
- · - 1 tbsp apple cider vinegar
- · - Salt and pepper to taste

DIRECTIONS

1. In a large bowl, combine sliced cucumbers, red onion, and dill.

2. In a separate bowl, mix sour cream (or Greek yogurt), apple cider vinegar, salt, and pepper.

3. Pour the dressing over the cucumber mixture and toss to combine.

4. Chill in the refrigerator for 15-30 minutes before serving.

Keto Cucumber Roll-Ups

INGREDIENTS

- · - 2 large cucumbers, sliced thinly lengthwise
- · - 1/2 cup cream cheese, softened
- · - 1/4 cup smoked salmon or deli meat (like turkey or ham)
- · - 1 tbsp fresh chives, chopped
- · - Salt and pepper to taste

DIRECTIONS

1. Lay cucumber slices flat on a cutting board.

2. Spread a thin layer of cream cheese on each slice.

3. Place a slice of smoked salmon or deli meat on top, followed by a sprinkle of chives, salt, and pepper.

4. Roll up each cucumber slice tightly and secure with a toothpick if needed.

5. Serve as a refreshing appetizer or snack.

Keto Cucumber and Avocado Salad

INGREDIENTS

- · - 2 large cucumbers, diced
- · - 1 ripe avocado, diced
- · - 1/4 cup red onion, finely chopped
- · - 1/4 cup chopped fresh cilantro
- · - 2 tbsp lime juice
- · - Salt and pepper to taste

DIRECTIONS

1. In a bowl, combine diced cucumbers, avocado, red onion, and cilantro.

2. Drizzle with lime juice and season with salt and pepper.

3. Gently toss to combine and serve immediately.

Keto Cucumber Salsa

INGREDIENTS
- · - 2 large cucumbers, diced
- · - 1/2 red onion, finely chopped
- · - 1 bell pepper (any color), diced
- · - 1 jalapeño, seeded and minced (optional)
- · - 1/4 cup chopped fresh cilantro
- · - 2 tbsp lime juice
- · - Salt and pepper to taste

DIRECTIONS
1. In a bowl, combine diced cucumbers, red onion, bell pepper, jalapeño, and cilantro.
2. Drizzle with lime juice and season with salt and pepper.
3. Toss to combine and serve as a refreshing salsa with grilled meats or as a dip with low-carb chips.

Keto Cucumber Hummus

INGREDIENTS
- · - 1 large cucumber, peeled and diced
- · - 1/2 cup tahini
- · - 1 garlic clove, minced
- · - 2 tbsp lemon juice
- · - 2 tbsp olive oil
- · - Salt and pepper to taste

DIRECTIONS
1. In a food processor, combine diced cucumber, tahini, garlic, lemon juice, olive oil, salt, and pepper.
2. Blend until smooth, adding a little water if needed to achieve desired consistency.
3. Serve as a dip with vegetable sticks or low-carb crackers.

Keto Almond Flour Rolls

INGREDIENTS
- · - 2 cups almond flour
- · - 2 tsp baking powder
- · - 1/2 tsp salt
- · - 2 large eggs
- · - 1/4 cup melted butter
- · - 1/4 cup shredded cheese (optional, for flavor)

DIRECTIONS
1. Preheat the oven to 350°F (175°C) and line a baking sheet with parchment paper.
2. In a bowl, mix almond flour, baking powder, and salt.
3. In another bowl, whisk the eggs and melted butter together.
4. Combine the wet and dry ingredients, mixing until a dough forms. If using, fold in the shredded cheese.
5. Divide the dough into 6-8 equal portions and shape them into rolls. Place them on the prepared baking sheet.
6. Bake for 15-20 minutes until golden brown. Let cool before serving.

Keto Cloud Bread Rolls

INGREDIENTS

- · - 3 large eggs
- · - 3 oz cream cheese, softened
- · - 1/4 tsp cream of tartar
- · - Salt to taste

DIRECTIONS

1. Preheat the oven to 300°F (150°C) and line a baking sheet with parchment paper.
2. Separate the egg whites from the yolks. In a bowl, beat the egg whites with cream of tartar until stiff peaks form.
3. In another bowl, mix the egg yolks, cream cheese, and salt until smooth.
4. Gently fold the egg whites into the yolk mixture until combined.
5. Spoon the mixture into the shape of rolls on the prepared baking sheet.
6. Bake for 25-30 minutes until golden brown and set. Let cool before serving.

Keto Flaxseed Rolls

INGREDIENTS

- · - 1 cup ground flaxseed meal
- · - 1/2 cup almond flour
- · - 1 tbsp baking powder
- · - 1/2 tsp salt
- · - 3 large eggs
- · - 1/4 cup melted coconut oil or butter
- · - 1/2 cup water

DIRECTIONS

1. Preheat the oven to 350°F (175°C) and line a baking sheet with parchment paper.
2. In a bowl, mix ground flaxseed, almond flour, baking powder, and salt.
3. In another bowl, whisk together the eggs, melted coconut oil (or butter), and water.
4. Combine the wet and dry ingredients, mixing until a dough forms.
5. Shape the dough into rolls and place them on the baking sheet.
6. Bake for 20-25 minutes until golden brown. Allow to cool before serving.

Keto Cheddar Cheese Rolls

INGREDIENTS

- · - 2 cups almond flour
- · - 1 tsp baking powder
- · - 1/2 tsp salt
- · - 1/4 cup shredded cheddar cheese
- · - 2 large eggs
- · - 1/4 cup melted butter

DIRECTIONS

. Preheat the oven to 350°F (175°C) and line a baking sheet with parchment paper.
2. In a bowl, mix almond flour, baking powder, salt, and shredded cheddar cheese.
3. In another bowl, whisk the eggs and melted butter together.
4. Combine the wet and dry ingredients, mixing until a dough forms.
5. Shape the dough into rolls and place them on the baking sheet.
6. Bake for 15-20 minutes until golden brown. Let cool before serving.

Keto Parmesan Garlic Rolls

INGREDIENTS
- · - 1 cup almond flour
- · - 1/2 cup shredded mozzarella cheese
- · - 1/4 cup grated Parmesan cheese
- · - 1 large egg
- · - 1 tsp garlic powder
- · - 1/2 tsp baking powder
- · - 1/2 tsp salt

DIRECTIONS
1. Preheat the oven to 350°F (175°C) and line a baking sheet with parchment paper.
2. In a bowl, combine almond flour, mozzarella cheese, Parmesan cheese, garlic powder, baking powder, and salt.
3. Add the egg and mix until a dough forms.
4. Shape the dough into small rolls and place them on the baking sheet.
5. Bake for 15-20 minutes until golden and cooked through. Let cool before serving.

Keto Cauliflower Rice Sushi Rolls

INGREDIENTS
- · - 2 cups cauliflower rice (fresh or frozen)
- · - 1 tbsp rice vinegar
- · - 1 tsp sesame oil
- · - 4 sheets nori (seaweed)
- · - 1/2 avocado, sliced
- · - 1/2 cucumber, julienned
- · - 1/2 cup cooked shrimp or crab meat (optional)
- · - Soy sauce or tamari for dipping

DIRECTIONS
1. If using fresh cauliflower, pulse it in a food processor until it resembles rice. If using frozen, thaw and drain excess moisture.
2. In a bowl, mix cauliflower rice with rice vinegar and sesame oil.
3. Place a sheet of nori on a bamboo sushi mat or parchment paper. Spread a thin layer of cauliflower rice over the nori, leaving about an inch at the top.
4. Arrange avocado, cucumber, and shrimp (if using) in a line across the center of the rice.
5. Roll the sushi tightly from the bottom, using the mat to help shape it. Seal the edge with a little water.
6. Slice into pieces and serve with soy sauce or tamari for dipping.

Keto Salmon Avocado Rolls

INGREDIENTS
- · - 4 oz smoked salmon
- · - 1/2 avocado, sliced
- · - 1/4 cucumber, julienned
- · - 1 tbsp cream cheese
- · - 2 sheets nori (seaweed)
- · - Soy sauce or tamari for dipping

DIRECTIONS
1. Lay a sheet of nori on a cutting board or bamboo mat.
2. Spread a thin layer of cream cheese over the nori.

3. Arrange slices of smoked salmon, avocado, and cucumber in a line across the center of the nori.
4. Roll the nori tightly from the bottom, using the mat to help shape it. Seal the edge with a little water.
5. Slice the roll into bite-sized pieces and serve with soy sauce or tamari.

Keto Tuna Salad Sushi

INGREDIENTS
- · - 1 can (5 oz) tuna, drained
- · - 2 tbsp mayonnaise
- · - 1 tsp Dijon mustard
- · - 1 tbsp chopped green onions
- · - 1/2 avocado, sliced
- · - 2 sheets nori (seaweed)

DIRECTIONS
1. In a bowl, mix tuna, mayonnaise, Dijon mustard, and green onions until well combined.
2. Lay a sheet of nori on a cutting board or bamboo mat.
3. Spread the tuna mixture evenly across the nori, leaving about an inch at the top.
4. Arrange slices of avocado on top of the tuna mixture.
5. Roll the nori tightly from the bottom, sealing the edge with water.
6. Slice into bite-sized pieces and enjoy!

Keto Cucumber Sushi Rolls

INGREDIENTS
- · - 2 large cucumbers
- · - 4 oz cream cheese, softened
- · - 1/2 cup cooked shrimp or crab meat
- · - 1/4 avocado, sliced
- · - 1/4 bell pepper, julienned
- · - Soy sauce or tamari for dipping

DIRECTIONS
1. Cut the cucumbers in half lengthwise and scoop out the seeds to create a hollow center.
2. In a bowl, mix cream cheese with shrimp or crab meat.
3. Fill each cucumber half with the cream cheese mixture.
4. Add avocado and bell pepper slices on top.
5. Slice the cucumbers into bite-sized pieces and serve with soy sauce or tamari.

Keto Spicy Tuna Roll

INGREDIENTS
- · - 1 can (5 oz) tuna, drained
- · - 1 tbsp mayonnaise
- · - 1 tsp Sriracha sauce (adjust to taste)
- · - 1/2 avocado, sliced
- · - 1/4 cucumber, julienned
- · - 2 sheets nori (seaweed)

DIRECTIONS
1. In a bowl, mix tuna, mayonnaise, and Sriracha until well combined.
2. Lay a sheet of nori on a cutting board or bamboo mat.
3. Spread the spicy tuna mixture evenly across the nori, leaving about an inch at the top.

4. Arrange slices of avocado and cucumber on top of the tuna mixture.

5. Roll the nori tightly from the bottom, sealing the edge with water.

6. Slice into bite-sized pieces and serve with soy sauce or tamari.

Keto Cauliflower Fried Rice

INGREDIENTS

- · - 1 medium head of cauliflower, riced (or 4 cups pre-riced cauliflower)
- · - 2 tbsp sesame oil (or olive oil)
- · - 2 eggs, beaten
- · - 1/2 cup green peas (optional, use sparingly for carbs)
- · - 1/2 cup carrots, diced (optional, use sparingly for carbs)
- · - 3 green onions, chopped
- · - 3 tbsp soy sauce or tamari
- · - 1 tsp garlic, minced
- · - Salt and pepper to taste

DIRECTIONS

1. In a large skillet or wok, heat sesame oil over medium heat.

2. Add the garlic and sauté for 1 minute until fragrant.

3. Push the garlic to the side and scramble the beaten eggs until cooked. Mix with the garlic.

4. Add the riced cauliflower to the skillet along with peas and carrots if using. Stir-fry for about 5-7 minutes until the cauliflower is tender.

5. Stir in soy sauce, green onions, and season with salt and pepper. Cook for another 2-3 minutes.

6. Serve hot as a side dish or main course.

Keto Broccoli Rice Casserole

INGREDIENTS

- · - 4 cups broccoli florets, chopped finely (or riced)
- · - 1 cup shredded cheddar cheese
- · - 1/2 cup cream cheese, softened
- · - 1/2 cup chicken broth
- · - 2 large eggs
- · - 1/2 tsp garlic powder
- · - Salt and pepper to taste

DIRECTIONS

1. Preheat the oven to 350°F (175°C). Grease a baking dish.

2. In a large bowl, combine chopped broccoli, cream cheese, chicken broth, eggs, garlic powder, salt, and pepper. Mix well.

3. Fold in 3/4 cup of shredded cheddar cheese.

4. Pour the mixture into the greased baking dish and top with the remaining cheese.

5. Bake for 25-30 minutes until the casserole is set and the cheese is bubbly and golden.

6. Let cool slightly before serving.

Keto Mushroom Risotto (Cauliflower Rice)

INGREDIENTS

- · - 2 cups cauliflower rice
- · - 1 cup mushrooms, sliced
- · - 1/4 cup onion, diced
- · - 2 cloves garlic, minced
- · - 1/2 cup chicken or vegetable broth
- · - 1/4 cup heavy cream
- · - 1/4 cup grated Parmesan cheese
- · - 2 tbsp olive oil
- · - Salt and pepper to taste
- · - Fresh parsley for garnish

DIRECTIONS

1. In a skillet, heat olive oil over medium heat. Add onions and garlic; sauté until translucent.

2. Add mushrooms and cook until they are soft and browned.

3. Stir in cauliflower rice and broth. Cook for about 5-7 minutes until the cauliflower is tender.

4. Reduce heat to low and stir in heavy cream and Parmesan cheese. Cook for an additional 2-3 minutes.

5. Season with salt and pepper and garnish with fresh parsley before serving.

Keto Jicama Rice Bowl

INGREDIENTS

- · - 1 medium jicama, peeled and riced (or store-bought jicama rice)
- · - 1 lb ground beef or turkey
- · - 1 bell pepper, diced
- · - 1/2 onion, diced
- · - 2 cloves garlic, minced
- · - 1 tsp chili powder
- · - 1 tsp cumin
- · - Salt and pepper to taste
- · - Avocado and cilantro for topping

DIRECTIONS

1. In a skillet, brown the ground meat over medium heat. Drain excess fat if necessary.

2. Add onion, bell pepper, and garlic, cooking until the vegetables are tender.

3. Stir in chili powder, cumin, salt, and pepper. Mix well.

4. In a separate skillet, lightly sauté riced jicama in a little olive oil for 2-3 minutes until slightly tender.

5. Serve the meat mixture over the jicama rice and top with avocado and cilantro.

Keto Eggplant "Rice" Bowl

INGREDIENTS

- · - 1 large eggplant, diced
- · - 1 cup cooked chicken or shrimp
- · - 1/2 cup diced tomatoes
- · - 1/2 onion, diced
- · - 2 cloves garlic, minced
- · - 2 tbsp olive oil
- · - Italian seasoning to taste
- · - Salt and pepper to taste
- · - Fresh basil for garnish

DIRECTIONS

1. In a skillet, heat olive oil over medium heat. Add onion and garlic; sauté until translucent.

2. Add diced eggplant and cook until softened, about 5-7 minutes.

3. Stir in cooked chicken or shrimp, diced tomatoes, Italian seasoning, salt, and pepper. Cook until heated through.

4. Serve warm, garnished with fresh basil.

Keto Chocolate Avocado Mousse

INGREDIENTS
- · - 1 ripe avocado
- · - 1/4 cup unsweetened cocoa powder
- · - 1/4 cup almond milk (or coconut milk)
- · - 1/4 cup erythritol or your preferred sweetener
- · - 1 tsp vanilla extract
- · - Pinch of salt

DIRECTIONS

1. In a blender or food processor, combine the avocado, cocoa powder, almond milk, erythritol, vanilla extract, and salt.

2. Blend until smooth and creamy, scraping down the sides as needed.

3. Taste and adjust sweetness if necessary.

4. Chill in the refrigerator for at least 30 minutes before serving. Enjoy as a rich dessert!

Keto Chocolate Chip Cookies

INGREDIENTS
- · - 2 cups almond flour
- · - 1/2 cup erythritol or your preferred sweetener
- · - 1/2 tsp baking soda
- · - 1/2 tsp salt
- · - 1/2 cup unsalted butter, softened
- · - 1 large egg
- · - 1 tsp vanilla extract
- · - 1/2 cup sugar-free chocolate chips

DIRECTIONS

1. Preheat the oven to 350°F (175°C) and line a baking sheet with parchment paper.

2. In a bowl, mix almond flour, erythritol, baking soda, and salt.

3. In another bowl, cream together the butter, egg, and vanilla extract.

4. Combine the wet and dry ingredients, then fold in the chocolate chips.

5. Scoop tablespoon-sized portions onto the baking sheet, spacing them apart.

6. Bake for 10-12 minutes until golden. Let cool before serving.

Keto Chocolate Fat Bombs

INGREDIENTS
- · - 1/2 cup coconut oil, melted
- · - 1/2 cup unsweetened cocoa powder
- · - 1/4 cup almond butter (or peanut butter)
- · - 1/4 cup erythritol or your preferred sweetener
- · - 1 tsp vanilla extract
- · - A pinch of salt

DIRECTIONS

1. In a mixing bowl, combine melted coconut oil, cocoa powder, almond butter, erythritol, vanilla extract, and salt. Mix until smooth.
2. Pour the mixture into silicone molds or a lined muffin tin.
3. Freeze for about 30 minutes until solid.
4. Pop out the fat bombs and store them in the freezer for a quick snack.

Keto Chocolate Chia Pudding

INGREDIENTS
- - 1/4 cup chia seeds
- - 1 cup unsweetened almond milk (or coconut milk)
- - 2 tbsp unsweetened cocoa powder
- - 2 tbsp erythritol or your preferred sweetener
- - 1 tsp vanilla extract
- - A pinch of salt

DIRECTIONS

1. In a bowl, whisk together almond milk, cocoa powder, erythritol, vanilla extract, and salt.
2. Stir in chia seeds until well combined.
3. Refrigerate for at least 2 hours or overnight until the mixture thickens to a pudding-like consistency.
4. Serve chilled, topped with berries or nuts if desired.

Keto Chocolate Zucchini Bread

INGREDIENTS
- - 1 1/2 cups almond flour
- - 1/2 cup unsweetened cocoa powder
- - 1/2 cup erythritol or your preferred sweetener
- - 1 tsp baking soda
- - 1/2 tsp salt,3 large eggs
- - 1 cup grated zucchini (squeeze out excess moisture)
- - 1/4 cup melted coconut oil or butter
- - 1 tsp vanilla extract
- - 1/2 cup sugar-free chocolate chips (optional)

DIRECTIONS

1. Preheat the oven to 350°F (175°C) and grease a loaf pan.
2. In a bowl, mix almond flour, cocoa powder, erythritol, baking soda, and salt.
3. In another bowl, whisk together eggs, grated zucchini, melted oil, and vanilla extract.
4. Combine wet and dry ingredients until well mixed. Fold in chocolate chips if using.
5. Pour the batter into the prepared loaf pan.
6. Bake for 45-55 minutes or until a toothpick comes out clean. Let cool before slicing.

Keto Almond Flour Pancakes

INGREDIENTS
- - 1 cup almond flour
- - 2 large eggs
- - 1/4 cup unsweetened almond milk (or coconut milk)
- - 1 tsp baking powder
- - 1/2 tsp vanilla extract
- - Pinch of salt

· - Butter or oil for cooking

DIRECTIONS

1. In a bowl, whisk together almond flour, baking powder, and salt.
2. In another bowl, beat the eggs and mix in almond milk and vanilla extract.
3. Combine the wet and dry ingredients until a batter forms.
4. Heat a non-stick skillet over medium heat and add butter or oil.
5. Pour about 1/4 cup of batter for each pancake into the skillet.
6. Cook for 2-3 minutes until bubbles form, then flip and cook for an additional 1-2 minutes until golden brown.
7. Serve with sugar-free syrup or berries.

Keto Cream Cheese Pancakes

INGREDIENTS

· - 4 oz cream cheese, softened
· - 2 large eggs
· - 1/2 tsp baking powder
· - 1/2 tsp vanilla extract
· - Pinch of salt
· - Butter or oil for cooking

DIRECTIONS

1. In a bowl, blend cream cheese, eggs, baking powder, vanilla extract, and salt until smooth.
2. Heat a non-stick skillet over medium heat and add butter or oil.
3. Pour small amounts of batter (about 2-3 tablespoons) into the skillet for each pancake.
4. Cook for 2-3 minutes until golden, then flip and cook for another 1-2 minutes.
5. Serve warm with your favorite keto-friendly toppings.

Keto Coconut Flour Pancakes

INGREDIENTS

· - 1/4 cup coconut flour
· - 3 large eggs
· - 1/4 cup unsweetened almond milk (or coconut milk)
· - 1 tsp baking powder
· - 1/2 tsp vanilla extract
· - 1/4 tsp salt
· - Butter or oil for cooking

DIRECTIONS

1. In a bowl, mix coconut flour, baking powder, and salt.
2. In another bowl, whisk the eggs, almond milk, and vanilla extract.
3. Combine the wet and dry ingredients until well mixed. Let the batter sit for a few minutes to thicken.
4. Heat a non-stick skillet over medium heat and add butter or oil.
5. Pour about 1/4 cup of batter for each pancake into the skillet.
6. Cook for 2-3 minutes until edges look set, then flip and cook for another 1-2 minutes.
7. Serve with sugar-free syrup or fresh berries.

Keto Chocolate Pancakes

INGREDIENTS

- · - 1 cup almond flour
- · - 1/4 cup unsweetened cocoa powder
- · - 2 large eggs
- · - 1/4 cup unsweetened almond milk (or coconut milk)
- · - 1 tsp baking powder
- · - 1/2 tsp vanilla extract
- · - Pinch of salt
- · - Butter or oil for cooking

DIRECTIONS

1. In a bowl, mix almond flour, cocoa powder, baking powder, and salt.

2. In another bowl, whisk the eggs, almond milk, and vanilla extract.

3. Combine the wet and dry ingredients until a smooth batter forms.

4. Heat a non-stick skillet over medium heat and add butter or oil.

5. Pour about 1/4 cup of batter for each pancake into the skillet.

6. Cook for 2-3 minutes until bubbles form, then flip and cook for another 1-2 minutes.

7. Serve with sugar-free chocolate syrup or whipped cream.

Keto Zucchini Pancakes

INGREDIENTS

- · - 1 cup grated zucchini (squeeze out excess moisture)
- · - 2 large eggs
- · - 1/4 cup almond flour
- · - 1/4 tsp garlic powder (optional)
- · - Salt and pepper to taste
- · - Butter or oil for cooking

DIRECTIONS

1. In a bowl, combine grated zucchini, eggs, almond flour, garlic powder, salt, and pepper.

2. Heat a non-stick skillet over medium heat and add butter or oil.

3. Pour small amounts of batter (about 2-3 tablespoons) into the skillet for each pancake.

4. Cook for 2-3 minutes until golden, then flip and cook for another 1-2 minutes.

5. Serve warm with sour cream or your favorite keto-friendly dip.

Keto Parmesan Crisps

INGREDIENTS

- · - 1 cup grated Parmesan cheese
- · - 1/2 tsp garlic powder (optional)
- · - 1/2 tsp Italian seasoning (optional)

DIRECTIONS

1. Preheat the oven to 400°F (200°C) and line a baking sheet with parchment paper.

2. In a bowl, mix the grated Parmesan cheese with garlic powder and Italian seasoning if using.

3. Scoop tablespoon-sized portions of the cheese mixture onto the baking sheet, spacing them apart.

4. Flatten each mound slightly with the back of a spoon.

5. Bake for 5-7 minutes until the edges are golden and crispy.

6. Allow to cool before serving as a snack or topping for salads.

Keto Parmesan Chicken

INGREDIENTS

- · - 4 boneless, skinless chicken breasts
- · - 1/2 cup grated Parmesan cheese
- · - 1/2 cup almond flour
- · - 1 tsp garlic powder
- · - 1 tsp Italian seasoning
- · - Salt and pepper to taste
- · - 2 large eggs
- · - Olive oil for frying

DIRECTIONS

1. In a shallow bowl, mix almond flour, Parmesan cheese, garlic powder, Italian seasoning, salt, and pepper.
2. In another bowl, beat the eggs.
3. Dip each chicken breast into the egg mixture, then coat with the Parmesan mixture.
4. Heat olive oil in a skillet over medium heat. Cook the chicken for about 5-7 minutes on each side until golden brown and cooked through.
5. Serve with a side of vegetables or salad.

Keto Parmesan Zucchini Noodles

INGREDIENTS

- · - 2 medium zucchini, spiralized into noodles
- · - 1/2 cup grated Parmesan cheese
- · - 2 tbsp olive oil
- · - 2 cloves garlic, minced
- · - Salt and pepper to taste
- · - Fresh basil for garnish (optional)

DIRECTIONS

1. In a large skillet, heat olive oil over medium heat. Add minced garlic and sauté for 1 minute.
2. Add the zucchini noodles and cook for 3-4 minutes until tender.
3. Remove from heat and stir in grated Parmesan cheese, salt, and pepper.
4. Serve immediately, garnished with fresh basil if desired.

Keto Parmesan Cauliflower Bake

INGREDIENTS

- · - 1 medium head of cauliflower, cut into florets
- · - 1/2 cup grated Parmesan cheese
- · - 1/2 cup heavy cream
- · - 1/2 cup shredded mozzarella cheese
- · - 1 tsp garlic powder
- · - Salt and pepper to taste
- · - Fresh parsley for garnish (optional)

DIRECTIONS

1. Preheat the oven to 375°F (190°C). Grease a baking dish.
2. Steam or boil the cauliflower florets until tender, then drain and pat dry.
3. In a bowl, combine heavy cream, garlic powder, salt, and pepper. Add the cauliflower and toss to coat.
4. Transfer the mixture to the baking dish and sprinkle with Parmesan and mozzarella cheese.
5. Bake for 20-25 minutes until bubbly and golden on top. Garnish with fresh parsley before serving.

Keto Parmesan and Spinach Stuffed Mushrooms

INGREDIENTS

- · - 12 large portobello or white mushrooms, stems removed
- · - 1 cup fresh spinach, chopped
- · - 1/2 cup grated Parmesan cheese
- · - 1/4 cup cream cheese, softened
- · - 2 cloves garlic, minced
- · - Salt and pepper to taste
- · - Olive oil for drizzling

DIRECTIONS

1. Preheat the oven to 375°F (190°C) and line a baking sheet with parchment paper.

2. In a skillet, sauté minced garlic in olive oil until fragrant. Add chopped spinach and cook until wilted.

3. In a bowl, mix the sautéed spinach, cream cheese, and grated Parmesan cheese until well combined. Season with salt and pepper.

4. Stuff each mushroom cap with the spinach mixture and place on the baking sheet.

5. Drizzle with olive oil and bake for 15-20 minutes until the mushrooms are tender and the tops are golden.

6. Serve warm as an appetizer or side dish.

Keto Breakfast Sausage Patties

INGREDIENTS

- · - 1 lb ground pork
- · - 1 tsp salt
- · - 1 tsp black pepper
- · - 1 tsp dried sage
- · - 1/2 tsp dried thyme
- · - 1/2 tsp garlic powder
- · - 1/2 tsp onion powder
- · - 1/4 tsp red pepper flakes (optional)

DIRECTIONS

1. In a large bowl, combine all ingredients.

2. Mix well until all spices are evenly incorporated into the meat.

3. Form the mixture into small patties (about 2 inches in diameter).

4. Heat a skillet over medium heat and cook the patties for 4-5 minutes on each side or until they are cooked through and golden brown.

5. Serve hot with eggs or your favorite keto-friendly sides.

Keto Italian Sausage

INGREDIENTS

- · - 1 lb ground pork
- · - 1 tsp salt
- · - 1 tsp black pepper
- · - 1 tbsp fennel seeds (crushed)
- · - 1 tsp paprika
- · - 1/2 tsp garlic powder
- · - 1/2 tsp onion powder
- · - 1/4 tsp red pepper flakes (optional)

DIRECTIONS

1. In a mixing bowl, add the ground pork and all the spices.

2. Mix until well combined.

3. Shape the mixture into sausage links or patties.

4. Preheat a grill or skillet over medium heat and cook the sausages for about 5-7 minutes on each side until fully cooked.

5. Serve in sandwiches, with vegetables, or on their own.

Keto Sausage and Veggie Skillet

INGREDIENTS

- · - 1 lb sausage (any variety, sliced)
- · - 1 cup bell peppers, chopped
- · - 1 cup zucchini, sliced
- · - 1/2 onion, sliced
- · - 2 tbsp olive oil
- · - Salt and pepper to taste

DIRECTIONS

1. In a large skillet, heat olive oil over medium heat.

2. Add the sliced sausage and cook until browned, about 5-7 minutes.

3. Add the bell peppers, zucchini, and onion to the skillet.

4. Season with salt and pepper, and sauté for an additional 5-7 minutes until the veggies are tender.

5. Serve hot as a hearty meal or as a side dish.

Keto Sausage Stuffed Peppers

INGREDIENTS

- · - 4 bell peppers, halved and seeded
- · - 1 lb ground sausage (pork or chicken)
- · - 1 cup cauliflower rice
- · - 1 cup shredded cheese (mozzarella or cheddar)
- · - 1 tsp Italian seasoning
- · - Salt and pepper to taste

DIRECTIONS

1. Preheat the oven to 375°F (190°C).

2. In a mixing bowl, combine ground sausage, cauliflower rice, cheese, Italian seasoning, salt, and pepper.

3. Stuff each bell pepper half with the sausage mixture.

4. Place the stuffed peppers in a baking dish and cover with foil.

5. Bake for 30-35 minutes or until the peppers are tender and the sausage is cooked through.

6. Remove from the oven and let cool slightly before serving.

Keto Stuffed Bell Peppers

INGREDIENTS

- · - 4 large bell peppers (any color)
- · - 1 lb ground beef or turkey
- · - 1 cup cauliflower rice
- · - 1 cup diced tomatoes (canned, drained)
- · - 1 cup shredded cheese (cheddar or mozzarella)
- · - 1 tsp Italian seasoning
- · - Salt and pepper to taste

DIRECTIONS

1. Heat olive oil in a large skillet over medium heat.
2. Add the sliced chicken and cook until browned and cooked through, about 5-7 minutes.
3. Add the bell peppers and onion to the skillet, along with chili powder, cumin, salt, and pepper.
4. Sauté until the vegetables are tender, about 5-7 minutes.
5. Serve with lime wedges and garnish with fresh cilantro.

Keto Bell Pepper Nachos

INGREDIENTS

- · - 2 large bell peppers, sliced into strips
- · - 1 lb ground beef or turkey
- · - 1 cup shredded cheese (cheddar or Mexican blend)
- · - 1/2 cup salsa
- · - 1/4 cup sliced jalapeños (optional)
- · - Sour cream (for serving)
- · - Chopped green onions (for garnish)

DIRECTIONS

1. Preheat the oven to 400°F (200°C).
2. In a skillet, cook the ground meat until browned. Drain any excess fat.
3. Line a baking sheet with parchment paper and arrange the bell pepper strips in a single layer.
4. Top the peppers with cooked meat, salsa, and shredded cheese.
5. Add jalapeños if desired.
6. Bake for 10-15 minutes or until the cheese is melted and bubbly.
7. Serve with sour cream and garnish with green onions.

Keto Cream Cheese Stuffed Peppers

INGREDIENTS

- · - 4 mini bell peppers (or jalapeños)
- · - 8 oz cream cheese, softened
- · - 1/2 cup shredded cheese (cheddar or pepper jack)
- · - 1/4 cup cooked bacon bits (optional)
- · - 1 tsp garlic powder
- · - Salt and pepper to taste

DIRECTIONS

1. Preheat the oven to 375°F (190°C).
2. Cut the mini peppers in half lengthwise and remove the seeds.
3. In a bowl, mix cream cheese, shredded cheese, bacon bits, garlic powder, salt, and pepper until well combined.
4. Stuff each pepper half with the cream cheese mixture.
5. Place on a baking sheet and bake for 15-20 minutes until heated through and slightly golden.
6. Serve warm as an appetizer or snack.

Keto Almond Flour Bread

INGREDIENTS

- · - 2 cups almond flour
- · - 1/4 cup coconut flour
- · - 1/4 cup psyllium husk powder
- · - 1 tbsp baking powder
- · - 1/2 tsp salt
- · - 5 large eggs
- · - 1/4 cup melted butter
- · - 1 cup warm water
- · - 1 tbsp apple cider vinegar

DIRECTIONS

1. Preheat the oven to 350°F (175°C) and line a loaf pan with parchment paper.

2. In a large bowl, mix almond flour, coconut flour, psyllium husk, baking powder, and salt.

3. In another bowl, whisk together the eggs, melted butter, warm water, and apple cider vinegar.

4. Combine wet and dry ingredients and mix until a dough forms.

5. Transfer the dough to the prepared loaf pan and smooth the top.

6. Bake for 60 minutes or until golden brown and a toothpick comes out clean.

7. Let cool before slicing.

Keto Cloud Bread

INGREDIENTS

- · - 3 large eggs
- · - 3 oz cream cheese, softened
- · - 1/4 tsp cream of tartar
- · - 1/4 tsp salt

DIRECTIONS

1. Preheat the oven to 300°F (150°C) and line a baking sheet with parchment paper.

2. Separate the egg whites and yolks into two bowls.

3. In the bowl with egg yolks, add cream cheese and mix until smooth.

4. In another bowl, beat the egg whites with cream of tartar and salt until stiff peaks form.

5. Gently fold the egg whites into the egg yolk mixture until combined.

6. Spoon the mixture onto the baking sheet in 6 mounds.

7. Bake for 25-30 minutes or until golden brown.

8. Let cool before using as bread replacements.

Keto Flaxseed Bread

INGREDIENTS

- · - 1 1/2 cups ground flaxseed meal
- · - 1/2 cup almond flour
- · - 1/4 cup psyllium husk powder
- · - 1 tbsp baking powder
- · - 1 tsp salt
- · - 5 large eggs
- · - 1/4 cup melted coconut oil
- · - 1 cup warm water

DIRECTIONS

1. Preheat the oven to 350°F (175°C) and grease a loaf pan.

2. In a large bowl, mix flaxseed meal, almond flour, psyllium husk, baking powder, and salt.

3. In another bowl, whisk the eggs, melted coconut oil, and warm water.

4. Combine the wet and dry ingredients and mix until a dough forms.

5. Pour the dough into the prepared loaf pan and smooth the top.

6. Bake for 45-50 minutes or until a toothpick comes out clean.

7. Allow to cool before slicing.

Keto Cheese Bread Sticks

INGREDIENTS

- · - 1 1/2 cups shredded mozzarella cheese
- · - 2 oz cream cheese
- · - 1 large egg
- · - 1 cup almond flour
- · - 1 tsp garlic powder
- · - 1 tsp Italian seasoning
- · - Salt to taste

DIRECTIONS

1. Preheat the oven to 400°F (200°C) and line a baking sheet with parchment paper.

2. In a microwave-safe bowl, combine mozzarella cheese and cream cheese. Microwave for about 1 minute until melted, then stir until smooth.

3. In a separate bowl, mix almond flour, egg, garlic powder, Italian seasoning, and salt.

4. Combine the cheese mixture with the dry ingredients and mix until a dough forms.

5. Shape the dough into sticks on the baking sheet.

6. Bake for 12-15 minutes or until golden brown.

7. Serve warm with marinara or your favorite dipping sauce.

Keto Scrambled Eggs with Spinach and Feta

INGREDIENTS

- · - 3 large eggs
- · - 1 cup fresh spinach, chopped
- · - 1/4 cup feta cheese, crumbled
- · - 1 tbsp olive oil
- · - Salt and pepper to taste

DIRECTIONS

1. Heat olive oil in a skillet over medium heat.

2. Add chopped spinach and sauté until wilted.

3. In a bowl, beat the eggs with salt and pepper.

4. Pour the eggs over the spinach and stir gently until scrambled.

5. Add feta cheese and cook for another minute until heated through. Serve warm.

Avocado and Bacon Egg Cups

INGREDIENTS

- · - 1 ripe avocado
- · - 2 large eggs
- · - 2 slices cooked bacon, crumbled
- · - Salt and pepper to taste

DIRECTIONS

1. Preheat the oven to 375°F (190°C).

2. Cut the avocado in half and remove the pit. Scoop out a bit more flesh to make room for the egg.

3. Place avocado halves in a baking dish and crack an egg into each half.

4. Sprinkle with crumbled bacon, salt, and pepper.

5. Bake for about 15-20 minutes, or until the egg is set to your liking. Serve warm.

Keto Chia Seed Pudding

INGREDIENTS

- · - 1/4 cup chia seeds
- · - 1 cup unsweetened almond milk
- · - 1/2 tsp vanilla extract
- · - 1-2 tbsp low-carb sweetener (like erythritol or stevia)

DIRECTIONS

1.In a bowl, mix chia seeds, almond milk, vanilla extract, and sweetener.

2. Stir well to combine.

3. Cover and refrigerate overnight.

4. In the morning, stir again and top with berries or nuts if desired.

Keto Pancakes

INGREDIENTS

- · - 1 cup almond flour
- · - 4 oz cream cheese, softened
- · - 3 large eggs
- · - 1 tsp baking powder
- · - 1/2 tsp vanilla extract
- · - Butter or oil for cooking

DIRECTIONS

1. In a bowl, mix almond flour, cream cheese, eggs, baking powder, and vanilla until smooth.

2. Heat a skillet over medium heat and add butter or oil.

3. Pour batter into the skillet, forming pancakes. Cook for 2-3 minutes on each side until golden brown.

4. Serve with sugar-free syrup or berries.

Egg Muffins with Vegetables and Cheese

INGREDIENTS

- · - 6 large eggs
- · - 1/2 cup bell peppers, diced
- · - 1/2 cup onions, diced
- · - 1 cup spinach, chopped
- · - 1/2 cup shredded cheese (cheddar or mozzarella)
- · - Salt and pepper to taste

DIRECTIONS

1. Preheat the oven to 350°F (175°C) and grease a muffin tin.

2. In a bowl, whisk the eggs with salt and pepper.

3. Stir in diced bell peppers, onions, spinach, and shredded cheese.

4. Pour the mixture evenly into the muffin tin cups.

5. Bake for 20-25 minutes until set and lightly golden. Let cool before removing from the tin.

Keto Smoothie

INGREDIENTS

- · - 1 cup unsweetened almond milk
- · - 1/2 avocado
- · - 1 cup spinach
- · - 1 scoop protein powder (low-carb)
- · - 1-2 tbsp low-carb sweetener (optional)
- · - Ice cubes (optional)

DIRECTIONS

1. In a blender, combine almond milk, avocado, spinach, protein powder, and sweetener.

2. Blend until smooth. Add ice for a thicker texture if desired.

3. Pour into a glass and enjoy immediately.

Coconut Flour Porridge

INGREDIENTS

- · - 1/4 cup coconut flour
- · - 1 cup unsweetened almond milk
- · - 1/2 tsp cinnamon
- · - 1-2 tbsp low-carb sweetener
- · - Optional toppings: nuts, seeds, or berries

DIRECTIONS

1. In a saucepan, combine coconut flour, almond milk, cinnamon, and sweetener.

2. Cook over low heat, stirring constantly until the mixture thickens to your desired consistency.

3. Serve warm, topped with nuts, seeds, or berries if desired.

Keto Chicken Salad

INGREDIENTS

- · - 2 cups cooked chicken, shredded
- · - 1/4 cup mayonnaise
- · - 1 tbsp Dijon mustard
- · - 1/4 cup celery, diced
- · - 1/4 cup green onions, chopped
- · - Salt and pepper to taste
- · - Lettuce leaves for serving

DIRECTIONS

1. **Combine Ingredients**: In a large bowl, add the shredded chicken, mayonnaise, Dijon mustard, diced celery, and chopped green onions.

2. **Mix**: Stir everything together until well combined.

3. **Season**: Add salt and pepper to taste, mixing again to incorporate.

4. **Serve**: Spoon the chicken salad onto lettuce leaves and wrap or serve on a plate.

Zucchini Noodles with Pesto and Grilled Shrimp

INGREDIENTS
- · - 2 medium zucchinis, spiralized
- · - 1 cup cooked shrimp, peeled and deveined
- · - 1/4 cup pesto (store-bought or homemade)
- · - 1 tbsp olive oil
- · - Salt and pepper to taste
- · - Grated Parmesan cheese (optional)

DIRECTIONS

1. **Heat Oil**: In a skillet, heat olive oil over medium heat.
2. **Sauté Zucchini**: Add the spiralized zucchini noodles and sauté for 2-3 minutes until slightly softened.
3. **Add Shrimp**: Stir in the cooked shrimp and pesto, tossing everything to combine.
4. **Season**: Cook for an additional 2 minutes and season with salt and pepper.
5. **Serve**: Plate the dish and top with grated Parmesan cheese if desired.

Keto Egg Salad Lettuce Wraps

INGREDIENTS
- · - 4 hard-boiled eggs, chopped
- · - 1/4 cup mayonnaise
- · - 1 tsp Dijon mustard
- · - 1/4 cup celery, diced
- · - Salt and pepper to taste
- · - Romaine or butter lettuce leaves for wrapping

DIRECTIONS

1. **Mix Ingredients**: In a bowl, combine the chopped hard-boiled eggs, mayonnaise, Dijon mustard, and diced celery.
2. **Season**: Add salt and pepper to taste and mix until smooth.
3. **Prepare Lettuce**: Wash and dry the lettuce leaves.
4. **Assemble**: Spoon the egg salad into the lettuce leaves and wrap them to serve.

Stuffed Bell Peppers

INGREDIENTS
- · - 2 large bell peppers, halved and seeded
- · - 1 lb ground beef or turkey
- · - 1 cup cauliflower rice
- · - 1/2 cup diced tomatoes (canned, drained)
- · - 1 tsp Italian seasoning
- · - 1 cup shredded cheese (mozzarella or cheddar)

DIRECTIONS

1. **Preheat Oven**: Preheat the oven to 375°F (190°C).
2. **Cook Meat**: In a skillet, cook the ground meat over medium heat until browned. Drain excess fat.
3. **Add Fillings**: Stir in cauliflower rice, diced tomatoes, and Italian seasoning. Mix until combined.
4. **Stuff Peppers**: Spoon the mixture into the halved bell peppers, placing them in a baking dish.
5. **Top with Cheese**: Sprinkle shredded cheese on top of each stuffed pepper.
6. **Bake**: Cover the dish with foil and bake for 30-35 minutes until the peppers are tender.

Keto Tuna Salad

INGREDIENTS
- - 1 can (5 oz) tuna, drained
- - 1/4 cup mayonnaise
- - 1 tbsp Dijon mustard
- - 1/4 cup celery, diced
- - 1/4 cup pickles, diced
- - Salt and pepper to taste
- - Lettuce leaves for serving

DIRECTIONS

1. **Combine Tuna**: In a bowl, add the drained tuna, mayonnaise, Dijon mustard, diced celery, and diced pickles.
2. **Mix**: Stir until all ingredients are well combined.
3. **Season**: Add salt and pepper to taste and mix again.
4. **Serve**: Serve on a bed of greens or in lettuce wraps.

Stuffed Bell Peppers

INGREDIENTS
- - 2 large bell peppers, halved and seeded
- - 1 lb ground beef or turkey
- - 1 cup cauliflower rice
- - 1/2 cup diced tomatoes (canned, drained)
- - 1 tsp Italian seasoning
- - 1 cup shredded cheese (mozzarella or cheddar)

DIRECTIONS

1. **Preheat Oven**: Preheat the oven to 375°F (190°C).
2. **Cook Meat**: In a skillet, cook the ground meat over medium heat until browned. Drain excess fat.
3. **Add Fillings**: Stir in cauliflower rice, diced tomatoes, and Italian seasoning. Mix until combined.
4. **Stuff Peppers**: Spoon the mixture into the halved bell peppers, placing them in a baking dish.
5. **Top with Cheese**: Sprinkle shredded cheese on top of each stuffed pepper.
6. **Bake**: Cover the dish with foil and bake for 30-35 minutes until the peppers are tender.

Keto Tuna Salad

INGREDIENTS
- - 1 can (5 oz) tuna, drained
- - 1/4 cup mayonnaise
- - 1 tbsp Dijon mustard
- - 1/4 cup celery, diced
- - 1/4 cup pickles, diced
- - Salt and pepper to taste
- - Lettuce leaves for serving

DIRECTIONS

1. **Combine Tuna**: In a bowl, add the drained tuna, mayonnaise, Dijon mustard, diced celery, and diced pickles.
2. **Mix**: Stir until all ingredients are well combined.
3. **Season**: Add salt and pepper to taste and mix again.
4. **Serve**: Serve on a bed of greens or in lettuce wraps.

Keto Cauliflower Fried Rice

INGREDIENTS

- · - 2 cups cauliflower rice
- · - 1/2 cup diced cooked chicken
- · - 1/4 cup peas (optional)
- · - 1/4 cup green onions, chopped
- · - 2 eggs, beaten
- · - 2 tbsp soy sauce (or coconut aminos)
- · - Olive oil for cooking

DIRECTIONS

1. **Heat Oil**: In a skillet, heat olive oil over medium heat.
2. **Add Cauliflower Rice**: Add cauliflower rice and cook for 3-4 minutes until slightly tender.
3. **Scramble Eggs**: Push the rice to one side of the skillet, add beaten eggs to the other side, and scramble until cooked.
4. **Combine**: Stir in diced chicken, peas, green onions, and soy sauce. Cook for another 2-3 minutes until everything is heated through.
5. **Serve**: Plate the cauliflower fried rice and enjoy warm.

Keto Chicken and Broccoli Casserole

INGREDIENTS

- · - 2 cups cooked chicken, shredded
- · - 2 cups broccoli florets, steamed
- · - 1 cup shredded cheese (cheddar or mozzarella)
- · - 1/2 cup heavy cream
- · - 1/2 tsp garlic powder
- · - Salt and pepper to taste

DIRECTIONS

1. **Preheat Oven**: Preheat the oven to 350°F (175°C).
2. **Mix Ingredients**: In a large bowl, combine shredded chicken, steamed broccoli, half of the cheese, heavy cream, garlic powder, salt, and pepper.
3. **Transfer to Baking Dish**: Pour the mixture into a baking dish and spread evenly.
4. **Top with Cheese**: Sprinkle the remaining cheese on top.
5. **Bake**: Bake for 25-30 minutes until bubbly and golden.

Keto Lemon Garlic Butter Shrimp

INGREDIENTS

- · - 1 lb large shrimp, peeled and deveined
- · - 4 tbsp butter
- · - 4 cloves garlic, minced
- · - Juice of 1 lemon
- · - Salt and pepper to taste
- · - Chopped parsley for garnish

DIRECTIONS

1. **Melt Butter**: In a large skillet, melt butter over medium heat.
2. **Add Garlic**: Add minced garlic and sauté for 1-2 minutes until fragrant.
3. **Cook Shrimp**: Add shrimp to the skillet, season with salt and pepper, and cook for 3-4 minutes until they turn pink.
4. **Add Lemon Juice**: Squeeze lemon juice over the shrimp and stir to combine.
5. **Garnish and Serve**: Garnish with chopped parsley and serve immediately.

Keto Chicken Alfredo with Zucchini Noodles

INGREDIENTS

- - 2 medium zucchinis, spiralized
- - 2 cups cooked chicken, shredded
- - 1 cup heavy cream
- - 1 cup grated Parmesan cheese
- - 2 tbsp butter
- - 2 cloves garlic, minced
- - Salt and pepper to taste
- - Fresh parsley for garnish

DIRECTIONS

1. **Cook Zucchini Noodles**: In a skillet, sauté spiralized zucchini noodles in a little olive oil for 2-3 minutes. Set aside.

2. **Make Alfredo Sauce**: In the same skillet, melt butter over medium heat, add minced garlic, and sauté for 1-2 minutes.

3. **Add Cream and Cheese**: Pour in heavy cream, bring to a simmer, and stir in Parmesan cheese until melted. Season with salt and pepper.

4. **Combine**: Add shredded chicken to the sauce and stir until heated through.

5. **Serve**: Serve the chicken Alfredo over zucchini noodles and garnish with parsley.

Keto Beef Stir-Fry

INGREDIENTS

- - 1 lb flank steak, sliced thinly
- - 2 cups mixed bell peppers, sliced
- - 1 cup broccoli florets
- - 3 tbsp soy sauce (or coconut aminos)
- - 2 tbsp olive oil
- - 2 cloves garlic, minced
- - 1 tsp ginger, grated

DIRECTIONS

1. **Heat Oil**: In a large skillet or wok, heat olive oil over high heat.

2. **Cook Beef**: Add sliced flank steak and cook for 2-3 minutes until browned. Remove and set aside.

3. **Stir-Fry Vegetables**: In the same skillet, add bell peppers, broccoli, garlic, and ginger. Stir-fry for 3-4 minutes until tender-crisp.

4. **Combine**: Return the beef to the skillet and pour in soy sauce. Stir to combine and cook for another minute.

5. **Serve**: Serve hot, garnished with sesame seeds if desired.

Keto Baked Salmon with Asparagus

INGREDIENTS

- - 2 salmon fillets
- - 1 lb asparagus, trimmed
- - 3 tbsp olive oil
- - 2 cloves garlic, minced
- - Juice of 1 lemon
- - Salt and pepper to taste
- - Lemon wedges for serving

DIRECTIONS

1. **Preheat Oven**: Preheat the oven to 400°F (200°C).
2. **Prepare Baking Sheet**: Line a baking sheet with parchment paper.
3. **Season Salmon and Asparagus**: Place salmon and asparagus on the baking sheet. Drizzle with olive oil, lemon juice, garlic, salt, and pepper. Toss the asparagus to coat.
4. **Bake**: Bake for 12-15 minutes or until the salmon is cooked through and flakes easily with a fork.
5. **Serve**: Serve with lemon wedges.

Keto Spinach and Mushroom Casserole

INGREDIENTS

- · - 1 lb mushrooms, sliced
- · - 3 cups fresh spinach
- · - 1 cup heavy cream
- · - 1 cup shredded cheese (cheddar or mozzarella)
- · - 1/2 cup grated Parmesan cheese
- · - 2 cloves garlic, minced
- · - 2 tbsp olive oil
- · - Salt and pepper to taste

DIRECTIONS

1. **Preheat Oven**: Preheat your oven to 375°F (190°C).
2. **Sauté Vegetables**: In a skillet, heat olive oil over medium heat. Add mushrooms and garlic, cooking until mushrooms are tender. Add spinach and cook until wilted.
3. **Mix Casserole**: In a mixing bowl, combine the sautéed vegetables, heavy cream, shredded cheese, salt, and pepper.
4. **Transfer to Baking Dish**: Pour the mixture into a greased baking dish and top with grated Parmesan cheese.
5. **Bake**: Bake for 20-25 minutes until bubbly and golden on top.
6. **Serve**: Allow to cool slightly before serving. Enjoy this comforting casserole!

Keto Cauliflower Mac and Cheese

INGREDIENTS

- · - 1 head of cauliflower, cut into florets
- · - 1 cup heavy cream
- · - 1 cup shredded cheddar cheese
- · - 1/2 cup cream cheese
- · - 1/2 tsp garlic powder
- · - Salt and pepper to taste
- · - 1/4 cup grated Parmesan cheese (optional)

DIRECTIONS

1. **Cook Cauliflower**: Steam or boil cauliflower florets until tender, then drain.
2. **Make Cheese Sauce**: In a saucepan, combine heavy cream, cream cheese, garlic powder, salt, and pepper. Heat over medium until melted and smooth.
3. **Add Cheddar**: Stir in shredded cheddar cheese until melted.
4. **Combine**: Add cooked cauliflower to the cheese sauce and stir to coat.
5. **Serve**: If desired, top with grated Parmesan cheese and serve warm.

Keto Chicken Parmesan

INGREDIENTS

- · - 2 chicken breasts, flattened
- · - 1 cup almond flour
- · - 1/2 cup grated Parmesan cheese
- · - 1 egg, beaten
- · - 1 cup marinara sauce (sugar-free)
- · - 1 cup shredded mozzarella cheese
- · - Olive oil for frying
- · - Salt and pepper to taste

DIRECTIONS

1. **Preheat Oven**: Preheat the oven to 375°F (190°C).

2. **Prepare Coating**: In a bowl, mix almond flour, Parmesan cheese, salt, and pepper. In another bowl, beat the egg.

3. **Coat Chicken**: Dip each chicken breast in the egg, then coat with the almond flour mixture.

4. **Fry Chicken**: Heat olive oil in a skillet over medium heat. Fry the chicken for 4-5 minutes on each side until golden brown.

5. **Assemble**: Transfer the chicken to a baking dish. Top each piece with marinara sauce and shredded mozzarella.

6. **Bake**: Bake for 15-20 minutes until the cheese is bubbly and golden. Serve hot.

Keto Creamy Garlic Tuscan Chicken

INGREDIENTS

- · - 4 chicken breasts
- · - 2 tbsp olive oil
- · - 4 cloves garlic, minced
- · - 1 cup heavy cream
- · - 1 cup spinach, chopped
- · - 1/2 cup sun-dried tomatoes, chopped
- · - 1/2 cup grated Parmesan cheese
- · - Salt and pepper to taste
- · - Fresh basil for garnish (optional)

DIRECTIONS

1. **Cook Chicken**: In a skillet, heat olive oil over medium heat. Season chicken breasts with salt and pepper, then cook for 5-7 minutes on each side until golden and cooked through. Remove and set aside.

2. **Make Sauce**: In the same skillet, add minced garlic and sauté for 1 minute. Pour in heavy cream and bring to a simmer.

3. **Add Spinach and Tomatoes**: Stir in chopped spinach and sun-dried tomatoes, cooking until the spinach wilts.

4. **Add Cheese**: Stir in Parmesan cheese until melted and the sauce thickens.

5. **Combine**: Return the chicken to the skillet, coating it with the sauce.

6. **Serve**: Garnish with fresh basil if desired and serve hot.

Keto Beef Stroganoff

INGREDIENTS

- · - 1 lb beef sirloin, sliced thinly
- · - 2 tbsp olive oil
- · - 1 cup mushrooms, sliced
- · - 1 medium onion, diced
- · - 3 cloves garlic, minced
- · - 1 cup beef broth
- · - 1 cup heavy cream
- · - 1 tsp Dijon mustard
- · - Salt and pepper to taste
- · - Fresh parsley for garnish

DIRECTIONS

1. **Cook Beef**: In a large skillet, heat olive oil over medium-high heat. Add the sliced beef and cook until browned. Remove and set aside.
2. **Sauté Vegetables**: In the same skillet, add onions and mushrooms. Sauté until tender, then add garlic and cook for another minute.
3. **Add Broth**: Pour in beef broth, scraping the bottom of the skillet to deglaze. Bring to a simmer.
4. **Stir in Cream**: Lower the heat, add heavy cream and Dijon mustard, stirring until well combined. Let simmer until thickened.
5. **Combine**: Return the beef to the skillet and heat through. Season with salt and pepper.
6. **Serve**: Garnish with fresh parsley and serve over cauliflower rice or zucchini noodles.

Keto Baked Lemon Herb Salmon

INGREDIENTS

- · - 2 salmon fillets
- · - 2 tbsp olive oil
- · - Juice of 1 lemon
- · - 1 tsp garlic powder
- · - 1 tsp dried oregano
- · - Salt and pepper to taste
- · - Lemon slices for garnish

DIRECTIONS

1. **Preheat Oven**: Preheat the oven to 400°F (200°C).
2. **Prepare Marinade**: In a small bowl, mix olive oil, lemon juice, garlic powder, oregano, salt, and pepper.
3. **Marinate Salmon**: Place salmon fillets in a baking dish and pour the marinade over them, ensuring they are well coated.
4. **Bake**: Bake for 12-15 minutes or until salmon flakes easily with a fork.
5. **Serve**: Garnish with lemon slices and serve with a side of steamed vegetables.

Keto Cauliflower Mac and Cheese

INGREDIENTS

- · - 1 head of cauliflower, cut into florets
- · - 1 cup heavy cream
- · - 1 cup shredded cheddar cheese
- · - 1/2 cup cream cheese
- · - 1/2 tsp garlic powder
- · - Salt and pepper to taste

·   - 1/4 cup grated Parmesan cheese (optional)

DIRECTIONS

1. **Cook Cauliflower**: Steam or boil cauliflower florets until tender, then drain.

2. **Make Cheese Sauce**: In a saucepan, combine heavy cream, cream cheese, garlic powder, salt, and pepper. Heat over medium until melted and smooth.

3. **Add Cheddar**: Stir in shredded cheddar cheese until melted.

4. **Combine**: Add cooked cauliflower to the cheese sauce and stir to coat.

5. **Serve**: If desired, top with grated Parmesan cheese and serve warm.

Keto Creamy Mushroom Soup

INGREDIENTS

·   - 1 lb mushrooms, sliced
·   - 1 medium onion, diced
·   - 3 cloves garlic, minced
·   - 4 cups chicken or vegetable broth
·   - 1 cup heavy cream
·   - 2 tbsp olive oil
·   - Salt and pepper to taste
·   - Fresh parsley for garnish

DIRECTIONS

1. **Sauté Vegetables**: In a large pot, heat olive oil over medium heat. Add diced onion and sauté until translucent. Add minced garlic and sliced mushrooms, cooking until the mushrooms are browned.

2. **Add Broth**: Pour in the chicken or vegetable broth and bring to a boil. Reduce heat and simmer for 15-20 minutes.

3. **Blend**: Use an immersion blender to puree the soup until smooth. Alternatively, transfer to a blender in batches.

4. **Add Cream**: Stir in heavy cream and season with salt and pepper. Heat through.

5. **Serve**: Garnish with fresh parsley and serve warm.

Keto Caprese Salad

INGREDIENTS

·   - 2 large tomatoes, sliced
·   - 8 oz fresh mozzarella cheese, sliced
·   - Fresh basil leaves
·   - 2 tbsp olive oil
·   - 1 tbsp balsamic vinegar
·   - Salt and pepper to taste

DIRECTIONS

1. **Layer Ingredients**: On a serving platter, alternate layers of tomato slices, mozzarella slices, and basil leaves.

2. **Drizzle Dressing**: In a small bowl, whisk together olive oil, balsamic vinegar, salt, and pepper. Drizzle over the salad.

3. **Serve**: Enjoy immediately as a fresh and flavorful first course.

Keto Avocado Soup

INGREDIENTS

- · - 2 ripe avocados, peeled and pitted
- · - 2 cups vegetable broth (low-sodium)
- · - 1/2 cup heavy cream
- · - 1 lime, juiced
- · - 2 cloves garlic
- · - Salt and pepper to taste
- · - Chopped cilantro for garnish

DIRECTIONS

1. **Blend Ingredients**: In a blender, combine avocados, vegetable broth, heavy cream, lime juice, garlic, salt, and pepper. Blend until smooth.
2. **Chill**: For a cold soup, refrigerate for at least 30 minutes.
3. **Serve**: Pour into bowls and garnish with chopped cilantro.

Keto Spinach and Artichoke Dip

INGREDIENTS

- · - 1 cup frozen spinach, thawed and drained
- · - 1 cup canned artichoke hearts, chopped
- · - 1/2 cup cream cheese, softened
- · - 1/2 cup sour cream
- · - 1/2 cup grated Parmesan cheese
- · - 1/2 cup shredded mozzarella cheese
- · - 2 cloves garlic, minced
- · - Salt and pepper to taste

DIRECTIONS

1. **Preheat Oven**: Preheat the oven to 350°F (175°C).
2. **Mix Ingredients**: In a bowl, combine spinach, artichokes, cream cheese, sour cream, Parmesan cheese, mozzarella cheese, minced garlic, salt, and pepper. Mix until well combined.
3. **Bake**: Transfer the mixture to a baking dish and bake for 20-25 minutes until bubbly and golden on top.
4. **Serve**: Serve warm with sliced vegetables or low-carb crackers.

Keto Shrimp Cocktail

INGREDIENTS

- · - 1 lb shrimp, peeled and deveined
- · - 1/4 cup mayonnaise
- · - 2 tbsp ketchup (sugar-free)
- · - 1 tbsp horseradish (adjust to taste)
- · - Juice of 1 lemon
- · - Salt and pepper to taste
- · - Lemon wedges for serving

DIRECTIONS

1. **Cook Shrimp**: In a pot of boiling salted water, cook shrimp for 2-3 minutes until they turn pink. Drain and cool.
2. **Make Sauce**: In a bowl, mix mayonnaise, ketchup, horseradish, lemon juice, salt, and pepper.
3. **Serve**: Arrange shrimp on a platter with the sauce on the side. Garnish with lemon wedges.

Keto Chicken Shawarma

INGREDIENTS

- · - 1.5 lbs chicken thighs, boneless and skinless
- · - 3 tbsp olive oil
- · - 2 tbsp lemon juice
- · - 4 cloves garlic, minced
- · - 2 tsp ground cumin
- · - 2 tsp ground coriander
- · - 1 tsp ground paprika
- · - 1 tsp ground turmeric
- · - 1/2 tsp cayenne pepper (optional)
- · - Salt and pepper to taste
- · - Fresh parsley for garnish

DIRECTIONS

1. **Marinate Chicken**: In a large bowl, combine olive oil, lemon juice, minced garlic, cumin, coriander, paprika, turmeric, cayenne pepper, salt, and pepper. Add chicken thighs and coat well. Cover and marinate in the refrigerator for at least 1 hour (or overnight for best results).

2. **Cook Chicken**: Preheat the grill or a skillet over medium-high heat. Grill or sauté the chicken thighs for 6-7 minutes on each side until cooked through and slightly charred. Remove and let rest.

3. **Slice**: Slice the chicken into thin strips.

4. **Serve**: Serve with a side of garlic sauce (see recipe below) and garnish with fresh parsley.

Keto Beef Shawarma

INGREDIENTS

- · - 1.5 lbs beef sirloin, thinly sliced
- · - 3 tbsp olive oil
- · - 2 tbsp apple cider vinegar
- · - 4 cloves garlic, minced
- · - 2 tsp ground cumin
- · - 2 tsp ground coriander
- · - 1 tsp ground paprika
- · - 1 tsp ground turmeric
- · - 1/2 tsp cayenne pepper (optional)
- · - Salt and pepper to taste

DIRECTIONS

1. **Marinate Beef**: In a bowl, mix olive oil, apple cider vinegar, minced garlic, cumin, coriander, paprika, turmeric, cayenne pepper, salt, and pepper. Add the sliced beef and coat well. Marinate for at least 1 hour in the refrigerator.

2. **Cook Beef**: Heat a skillet over medium-high heat. Add the marinated beef and cook for 3-4 minutes until browned and cooked through.

3. **Serve**: Serve with a side of tahini sauce (see recipe below) and garnish with chopped vegetables or salad.

Keto Shawarma Sauce

INGREDIENTS

- · - 1/2 cup mayonnaise
- · - 2 tbsp lemon juice
- · - 2 cloves garlic, minced
- · - Salt and pepper to taste

- - Water to thin (optional)

DIRECTIONS

1. **Mix Ingredients**: In a small bowl, combine mayonnaise, lemon juice, minced garlic, salt, and pepper.

2. **Adjust Consistency**: If the sauce is too thick, add a little water until you reach your desired consistency.

3. **Serve**: Drizzle over chicken or beef shawarma and enjoy!

Keto Shawarma Lettuce Wraps

INGREDIENTS

- - 1 batch of chicken or beef shawarma (from above)
- - Butter lettuce or romaine lettuce leaves
- - Chopped cucumbers
- - Sliced tomatoes
- - Sliced red onions
- - Fresh parsley for garnish

DIRECTIONS

1. **Prepare Wraps**: Place a slice of cooked shawarma in a lettuce leaf.

2. **Add Toppings**: Top with chopped cucumbers, sliced tomatoes, sliced red onions, and fresh parsley.

3. **Drizzle Sauce**: Drizzle with garlic sauce or tahini sauce.

4. **Wrap and Serve**: Roll up the lettuce leaf and enjoy as a low-carb wrap!

Keto Chicken Gyro with Pita Bread Alternative

INGREDIENTS

- - 1 lb chicken breast, sliced
- - 2 tbsp olive oil
- - 1 tbsp lemon juice
- - 2 tsp dried oregano
- - 2 tsp garlic powder
- - Salt and pepper to taste
- - Low-carb pita bread or lettuce wraps
- - Toppings: sliced cucumbers, tomatoes, red onions, and tzatziki sauce

DIRECTIONS

1. **Marinate Chicken**: In a bowl, mix olive oil, lemon juice, oregano, garlic powder, salt, and pepper. Add sliced chicken and marinate for at least 30 minutes.

2. **Cook Chicken**: Heat a skillet over medium-high heat and cook the marinated chicken for 5-7 minutes until cooked through and golden brown.

3. **Assemble**: Place the cooked chicken in low-carb pita bread or lettuce wraps. Top with sliced cucumbers, tomatoes, red onions, and tzatziki sauce.

4. **Serve**: Enjoy immediately.

Keto Falafel with Low-Carb Pita

INGREDIENTS

- - 1 cup cooked cauliflower rice (or 1 cup almond flour)
- - 1/4 cup parsley, chopped
- - 2 cloves garlic, minced
- - 1 tsp cumin, 1 tsp coriander

- Salt and pepper to taste
- 2 eggs, beaten, Olive oil for frying
- Low-carb pita bread or lettuce wraps
- Toppings: tahini sauce, sliced tomatoes, cucumbers

DIRECTIONS

1. **Mix Ingredients**: In a bowl, combine cauliflower rice (or almond flour), parsley, garlic, cumin, coriander, salt, pepper, and beaten eggs. Mix until well combined.
2. **Form Falafel**: Shape the mixture into small patties or balls.
3. **Fry Falafel**: Heat olive oil in a skillet over medium heat. Fry the falafel for about 3-4 minutes on each side until golden brown.
4. **Assemble**: Place the falafel in low-carb pita bread or lettuce wraps. Top with tahini sauce, sliced tomatoes, and cucumbers.
5. **Serve**: Enjoy warm.

Keto Beef Shawarma in Pita Bread Alternative

INGREDIENTS

- 1.5 lbs beef sirloin, thinly sliced
- 3 tbsp olive oil
- 2 tbsp apple cider vinegar
- 4 cloves garlic, minced
- 2 tsp ground cumin
- 2 tsp ground coriander
- 1 tsp ground paprika
- 1 tsp ground turmeric
- Salt and pepper to taste
- Low-carb pita bread or lettuce wraps
- Toppings: sliced cucumbers, tomatoes, onions, and tahini sauce

DIRECTIONS

1. **Marinate Beef**: In a bowl, mix olive oil, apple cider vinegar, minced garlic, cumin, coriander, paprika, turmeric, salt, and pepper. Add the sliced beef and coat well. Marinate for at least 1 hour in the refrigerator.
2. **Cook Beef**: Heat a skillet over medium-high heat. Add the marinated beef and cook for 3-4 minutes until browned and cooked through.
3. **Assemble**: Place the beef in low-carb pita bread or lettuce wraps. Top with sliced cucumbers, tomatoes, onions, and tahini sauce.
4. **Serve**: Enjoy immediately.

Keto Pizza Pita

INGREDIENTS

- Low-carb pita bread or almond flour flatbread
- 1/2 cup sugar-free marinara sauce
- 1 cup shredded mozzarella cheese
- Toppings: pepperoni, sliced bell peppers, olives, mushrooms
- Italian seasoning for garnish

DIRECTIONS

1. **Preheat Oven**: Preheat your oven to 400°F (200°C).
2. **Assemble Pizza**: Place low-carb pita on a baking sheet. Spread marinara sauce over the top, then sprinkle with mozzarella cheese and your choice of toppings.
3. **Bake**: Bake for about 10-12 minutes or until the cheese is melted and bubbly.

4. **Garnish and Serve**: Sprinkle with Italian seasoning and serve hot.

Keto Mediterranean Wraps

INGREDIENTS
- - Low-carb pita bread or almond flour tortillas
- - 1 cup cooked chicken or turkey, shredded
- - 1/2 cup feta cheese, crumbled
- - 1/2 cup chopped cucumbers
- - 1/2 cup diced tomatoes
- - 1/4 cup black olives, sliced
- - 2 tbsp olive oil
- - 1 tbsp red wine vinegar
- - Salt and pepper to taste

DIRECTIONS

1. **Mix Dressing**: In a small bowl, whisk together olive oil, red wine vinegar, salt, and pepper.

2. **Combine Filling**: In a large bowl, mix shredded chicken, feta cheese, cucumbers, tomatoes, and olives. Drizzle with the dressing and toss to combine.

3. **Assemble Wraps**: Place the mixture in low-carb pita bread or almond flour tortillas, fold, and wrap.

4. **Serve**: Enjoy immediately as a refreshing and hearty meal.

Keto Pumpkin Pie

INGREDIENTS
- - **Crust**:
- -1 1/2 cups almond flour
- - 1/4 cup coconut flour
- - 1/4 cup butter, melted,1 egg
- - 2 tbsp erythritol or your preferred sweetener,1/2 tsp salt,
- *Filling**:
- - 1 can (15 oz) pure pumpkin puree
- - 1/2 cup erythritol or your preferred sweetener
- - 1/2 cup heavy cream,3 large eggs
- - 1 tsp vanilla extract
- - 1 tsp cinnamon, - 1/2 tsp nutmeg
- - 1/4 tsp ginger,1/4 tsp salt

DIRECTIONS

1. **Preheat Oven**: Preheat your oven to 350°F (175°C).

2. **Make the Crust**: In a bowl, combine almond flour, coconut flour, melted butter, egg, erythritol, and salt. Mix until a dough forms. Press the dough into a 9-inch pie pan evenly across the bottom and up the sides. Prick the bottom with a fork.

3. **Pre-bake the Crust**: Bake the crust for 10-12 minutes until lightly golden. Remove from the oven and let cool.

4. **Prepare the Filling**: In a large bowl, mix pumpkin puree, erythritol, heavy cream, eggs, vanilla extract, cinnamon, nutmeg, ginger, and salt until well combined.

5. **Fill the Crust**: Pour the pumpkin filling into the pre-baked crust.

6. **Bake**: Bake for 45-50 minutes until the filling is set and a knife inserted in the center comes out clean.

7. **Cool and Serve**: Let the pie cool before slicing. Serve with whipped cream if desired.

Keto Chocolate Cream Pie

INGREDIENTS

- - **Crust**:
- -1 1/2 cups almond flour
- - 1/4 cup cocoa powder, - 1/4 cup butter, melted,- 2 tbsp erythritol or your preferred sweetener, - 1 egg,
- *Filling**:
- -1 cup heavy cream,- 1 cup unsweetened almond milk
- - 1/2 cup erythritol or your preferred sweetener, 1/4 cup cocoa powder
- - 2 tbsp cornstarch (or keto-friendly thickener)
- - 1 tsp vanilla extract,Pinch of salt
- **Topping**:
- -1 cup heavy whipping cream
- - 2 tbsp erythritol or your preferred sweetener
- - 1 tsp vanilla extract

DIRECTIONS

1. **Preheat Oven**: Preheat your oven to 350°F (175°C).

2. **Make the Crust**: In a bowl, combine almond flour, cocoa powder, melted butter, erythritol, and egg. Press the mixture into a 9-inch pie pan evenly across the bottom and up the sides.

3. **Bake the Crust**: Bake for 10-12 minutes until set. Remove and let cool.

4. **Prepare the Filling**: In a saucepan, whisk together heavy cream, almond milk, erythritol, cocoa powder, cornstarch, vanilla extract, and salt. Cook over medium heat, whisking continuously until the mixture thickens.

5. **Fill the Crust**: Pour the chocolate filling into the cooled crust and refrigerate for at least 2 hours to set.

6. **Make the Topping**: In a bowl, whip heavy cream, erythritol, and vanilla extract until soft peaks form.

7. **Top and Serve**: Spread the whipped cream over the cooled pie before serving.

Keto Lemon Meringue Pie

INGREDIENTS

- **Crust**
- - 1 1/2 cups almond flour
- - 1/4 cup butter, melted,1 egg
- - 2 tbsp erythritol or your preferred sweetener
- - 1/2 tsp salt
- *Filling**:
- - 3 large eggs, separated
- - 1/2 cup erythritol or your preferred sweetener
- - 1/2 cup fresh lemon juice
- - Zest of 1 lemon
- - 1/4 cup heavy cream
- *Meringue**:
- - 3 egg whites,1/4 tsp cream of tartar
- - 1/4 cup erythritol or your preferred sweetener

DIRECTIONS

1. **Preheat Oven**: Preheat your oven to 350°F (175°C).

2. **Make the Crust**: In a bowl, combine almond flour, melted butter, egg, erythritol, and salt. Press the mixture into a 9-inch pie pan evenly across the bottom and up the sides. Bake for 10-12 minutes until lightly golden. Let cool.

3. **Prepare the Filling**: In a bowl, whisk together egg yolks, erythritol, lemon juice, lemon zest, and heavy cream. Pour the mixture into the cooled crust and bake for 15-20 minutes until set.

4. **Make the Meringue**: In a clean bowl, beat egg whites and cream of tartar until soft peaks form. Gradually add erythritol and continue to beat until stiff peaks form.

5. **Top the Pie**: Spread meringue over the lemon filling, sealing the edges. Bake for an additional 10-12 minutes until the meringue is golden.

6. **Cool and Serve**: Allow the pie to cool before slicing and serving.

Keto Cheesecake

INGREDIENTS

- **Crust**:
- - 1 1/2 cups almond flour
- - 1/4 cup butter, melted
- - 2 tbsp erythritol or your preferred sweetener
- - 1/2 tsp vanilla extract
- *Filling**:
- - 16 oz cream cheese, softened
- - 3/4 cup erythritol or your preferred sweetener
- - 3 large eggs,
- -1 tsp vanilla extract
- - 1/2 cup sour cream
- - 1/4 cup lemon juice

DIRECTIONS

1. **Preheat Oven**: Preheat your oven to 325°F (160°C).

2. **Make the Crust**: In a bowl, combine almond flour, melted butter, erythritol, and vanilla extract. Press the mixture into the bottom of a 9-inch springform pan.

3. **Bake the Crust**: Bake for 10-12 minutes until golden. Remove and let cool.

4. **Prepare the Filling**: In a large bowl, beat cream cheese and erythritol until smooth. Add eggs one at a time, mixing well after each addition. Stir in vanilla extract, sour cream, and lemon juice.

5. **Fill the Crust**: Pour the filling over the cooled crust and smooth the top.

6. **Bake**: Bake for 45-50 minutes until set. Turn off the oven and let the cheesecake cool in the oven with the door slightly ajar.

7. **Chill and Serve**: Refrigerate for at least 4 hours before serving. Enjoy plain or with a low-carb topping.

Keto Beef and Mushroom Meat Pie

INGREDIENTS

- - **Crust**
- - 2 cups almond flour
- - 1/4 cup coconut flour
- - 1/2 cup butter, melted
- - 1 large egg,1/2 tsp salt
- - 1/4 tsp baking powder,
- Filling**:
- - 1 lb ground beef
- - 1 cup mushrooms, diced
- - 1 small onion, diced
- - 2 cloves garlic, minced,1/2 cup beef broth
- - 1 tbsp Worcestershire sauce (optional)

- Salt and pepper to taste
- 1 tsp thyme- 1 tsp rosemary

DIRECTIONS

1. **Preheat Oven**: Preheat your oven to 350°F (175°C).
2. **Make the Crust**: In a bowl, combine almond flour, coconut flour, melted butter, egg, salt, and baking powder. Mix until a dough forms. Press the dough into a 9-inch pie dish, covering the bottom and sides. Prick the bottom with a fork.
3. **Pre-bake the Crust**: Bake the crust for 10-12 minutes until slightly golden. Remove from the oven and let cool.
4. **Prepare the Filling**: In a skillet over medium heat, cook the ground beef until browned. Add onions, garlic, and mushrooms, cooking until softened. Stir in beef broth, Worcestershire sauce, thyme, rosemary, salt, and pepper. Simmer for 5-7 minutes.
5. **Fill the Crust**: Pour the beef mixture into the pre-baked crust, spreading it evenly.
6. **Bake**: Bake for an additional 20-25 minutes until the filling is hot and the crust is golden brown.
7. **Cool and Serve**: Let the pie cool for a few minutes before slicing. Serve warm.

Keto Chicken Pot Pie

INGREDIENTS

- **Crust**:
- 2 cups almond flour
- 1/4 cup coconut flour
- 1/2 cup butter, melted,1 large egg
- 1/2 tsp salt,1/2 tsp garlic powder
- **Filling**:
- 2 cups cooked chicken, shredded
- 1 cup cauliflower florets, steamed and chopped
- 1/2 cup celery, diced
- 1/2 cup carrots, diced (optional, use sparingly for keto)
- 1/2 cup chicken broth,1/2 cup heavy cream
- 1 tsp thyme - Salt and pepper to taste

DIRECTIONS

1. **Preheat Oven**: Preheat your oven to 375°F (190°C).
2. **Make the Crust**: In a bowl, mix almond flour, coconut flour, melted butter, egg, salt, and garlic powder until a dough forms. Press the dough into a 9-inch pie dish and prick the bottom with a fork.
3. **Pre-bake the Crust**: Bake the crust for 10-12 minutes until lightly golden. Remove from the oven and let cool.
4. **Prepare the Filling**: In a saucepan, combine chicken broth, heavy cream, thyme, salt, and pepper. Bring to a simmer. Add shredded chicken, cauliflower, celery, and carrots, stirring to combine. Cook for 5 minutes until heated through.
5. **Fill the Crust**: Pour the chicken mixture into the pre-baked crust, spreading it evenly.
6. **Bake**: Bake for an additional 20-25 minutes until the filling is hot and bubbly.
7. **Cool and Serve**: Let cool slightly before slicing and serving.

Keto Pork and Spinach Meat Pie

INGREDIENTS

- **Crust**:
- 2 cups almond flour
- 1/4 cup coconut flour
- 1/2 cup butter, melted

- - 1 large egg, 1/2 tsp salt
- - 1/4 tsp baking powder
- *Filling**:
- - 1 lb ground pork
- - 2 cups fresh spinach, chopped
- - 1 small onion, diced
- - 2 cloves garlic, minced
- - 1/2 cup cream cheese, softened
- - Salt and pepper to taste
- - 1 tsp Italian seasoning

DIRECTIONS

1. **Preheat Oven**: Preheat your oven to 350°F (175°C).
2. **Make the Crust**: In a bowl, combine almond flour, coconut flour, melted butter, egg, salt, and baking powder. Mix until a dough forms. Press the dough into a 9-inch pie dish and prick the bottom with a fork.
3. **Pre-bake the Crust**: Bake the crust for 10-12 minutes until slightly golden. Remove from the oven and let cool.
4. **Prepare the Filling**: In a skillet over medium heat, cook ground pork until browned. Add onions, garlic, and spinach, cooking until spinach is wilted. Remove from heat and stir in cream cheese, salt, pepper, and Italian seasoning until combined.
5. **Fill the Crust**: Pour the pork mixture into the pre-baked crust, spreading it evenly.
6. **Bake**: Bake for an additional 20-25 minutes until the filling is hot and the crust is golden brown.
7. **Cool and Serve**: Let the pie cool for a few minutes before slicing. Serve warm.

Keto Lamb and Feta Meat Pie

INGREDIENTS

- **Crust**:
- -2 cups almond flour
- - 1/4 cup coconut flour
- - 1/2 cup butter, melted
- - 1 large egg, 1/2 tsp salt
- - 1/4 tsp baking powder
- **Filling**:
- -1 lb ground lamb
- - 1/2 cup feta cheese, crumbled
- - 1 small onion, diced
- - 2 cloves garlic, minced
- - 1 tsp oregano
- - Salt and pepper to taste
- - 1/2 cup spinach, chopped (optional)

DIRECTIONS

1. **Preheat Oven**: Preheat your oven to 350°F (175°C).
2. **Make the Crust**: In a bowl, mix almond flour, coconut flour, melted butter, egg, salt, and baking powder until a dough forms. Press the dough into a 9-inch pie dish and prick the bottom with a fork.
3. **Pre-bake the Crust**: Bake the crust for 10-12 minutes until lightly golden. Remove from the oven and let cool.
4. **Prepare the Filling**: In a skillet over medium heat, cook ground lamb until browned. Add onion, garlic, oregano, salt, and pepper. Stir in feta cheese and spinach (if using) and cook until spinach is wilted.
5. **Fill the Crust**: Pour the lamb mixture into the pre-baked crust, spreading it evenly.
6. **Bake**: Bake for an additional 20-25 minutes until the filling is hot and the crust is golden brown.

7. **Cool and Serve**: Let cool slightly before slicing and serving.

Keto Classic Cheeseburger

INGREDIENTS
- · - 1 lb ground beef (80/20 for best flavor)
- · - Salt and pepper to taste
- · - 4 slices of cheddar cheese
- · - Lettuce leaves (for wrapping)
- · - Sliced tomatoes
- · - Sliced pickles
- · - Sliced onions
- · - Mustard and mayonnaise (optional)

DIRECTIONS

1. **Form Patties**: Divide the ground beef into 4 equal portions and shape them into patties. Make a slight indentation in the center of each patty to prevent it from puffing up during cooking. Season both sides with salt and pepper.
2. **Cook Patties**: Heat a grill or skillet over medium-high heat. Cook the patties for about 4-5 minutes on each side for medium doneness. In the last minute of cooking, add a slice of cheddar cheese on top of each patty and cover to melt.
3. **Assemble Burgers**: Use large lettuce leaves to wrap the patties. Add sliced tomatoes, pickles, onions, and condiments as desired.
4. **Serve**: Enjoy your keto cheeseburger wrapped in lettuce!

Keto Bacon Avocado Burger

INGREDIENTS
- · - 1 lb ground beef
- · - Salt and pepper to taste
- · - 4 slices of bacon, cooked until crispy
- · - 1 ripe avocado, sliced
- · - Lettuce leaves (for wrapping)
- · - Sliced tomatoes
- · - Mayonnaise (optional)

DIRECTIONS

1. **Form Patties**: Shape the ground beef into 4 patties and season with salt and pepper.
2. **Cook Patties**: Heat a grill or skillet over medium-high heat and cook the patties for 4-5 minutes on each side until cooked to your desired doneness.
3. **Assemble Burgers**: Use lettuce leaves as a wrap. Place the cooked patty on the lettuce, top with crispy bacon, avocado slices, and tomatoes. Add mayonnaise if desired.
4. **Serve**: Enjoy this flavorful burger with the creaminess of avocado!

Keto Mushroom Swiss Burger

INGREDIENTS
- · - 1 lb ground beef
- · - Salt and pepper to taste
- · - 1 cup mushrooms, sliced
- · - 4 slices of Swiss cheese
- · - 2 tbsp olive oil
- · - Lettuce leaves (for wrapping)

· - Garlic powder (optional)

DIRECTIONS

1. **Form Patties**: Shape the ground beef into 4 patties and season with salt, pepper, and garlic powder if using.

2. **Cook Patties**: Heat a grill or skillet over medium-high heat and cook the patties for 4-5 minutes on each side until cooked to your liking. In the last minute of cooking, top each patty with a slice of Swiss cheese.

3. **Sauté Mushrooms**: In a separate skillet, heat olive oil over medium heat. Add sliced mushrooms and sauté until browned and tender.

4. **Assemble Burgers**: Use lettuce leaves to wrap the patties. Top with sautéed mushrooms and serve.

5. **Serve**: Enjoy the rich flavors of this burger!

Keto BBQ Burger

INGREDIENTS

· - 1 lb ground beef
· - Salt and pepper to taste
· - 1/4 cup sugar-free BBQ sauce
· - 4 slices of cheddar cheese
· - Lettuce leaves (for wrapping)
· - Sliced red onion
· - Pickles (optional)

DIRECTIONS

1. **Form Patties**: Shape the ground beef into 4 patties and season with salt and pepper.

2. **Cook Patties**: Heat a grill or skillet over medium-high heat and cook the patties for 4-5 minutes on each side. In the last minute of cooking, brush each patty with sugar-free BBQ sauce and add a slice of cheddar cheese to melt.

3. **Assemble Burgers**: Use lettuce leaves to wrap the patties. Top with sliced red onion, pickles, and additional BBQ sauce if desired.

4. **Serve**: Enjoy your BBQ-flavored keto burger!

Keto Turkey Burger with Spinach and Feta

INGREDIENTS

· - 1 lb ground turkey
· - 1/2 cup feta cheese, crumbled
· - 1 cup fresh spinach, chopped
· - Salt and pepper to taste
· - Lettuce leaves (for wrapping)
· - Sliced tomatoes
· - Tzatziki sauce (optional)

DIRECTIONS

1. **Mix Ingredients**: In a bowl, combine ground turkey, crumbled feta, chopped spinach, salt, and pepper. Mix until well combined.

2. **Form Patties**: Shape the mixture into 4 patties.

3. **Cook Patties**: Heat a grill or skillet over medium-high heat and cook the patties for 4-5 minutes on each side until cooked through.

4. **Assemble Burgers**: Use lettuce leaves to wrap the patties. Top with sliced tomatoes and tzatziki sauce if desired.

5. **Serve**: Enjoy this Mediterranean-inspired turkey burger!

Garlic Butter Green Beans

INGREDIENTS

- · - 1 lb fresh green beans, trimmed
- · - 3 tbsp butter
- · - 3 cloves garlic, minced
- · - Salt and pepper to taste
- · - Lemon zest (optional)

DIRECTIONS

1. **Blanch Green Beans**: Bring a pot of salted water to a boil. Add green beans and cook for 3-4 minutes until bright green and tender-crisp. Drain and immediately transfer to ice water to stop cooking.

2. **Sauté**: In a skillet, melt butter over medium heat. Add minced garlic and sauté until fragrant (about 1 minute).

3. **Combine**: Drain the green beans and add them to the skillet. Toss to coat in the garlic butter and season with salt, pepper, and lemon zest if using.

4. **Serve**: Enjoy warm as a tasty side dish!

Cheesy Broccoli Casserole

INGREDIENTS

- · - 4 cups broccoli florets (fresh or frozen)
- · - 1 cup shredded cheddar cheese
- · - 1/2 cup sour cream
- · - 1/4 cup cream cheese, softened
- · - 1/2 tsp garlic powder
- · - Salt and pepper to taste

DIRECTIONS

1. **Preheat Oven**: Preheat your oven to 350°F (175°C).

2. **Steam Broccoli**: If using fresh broccoli, steam until tender. If using frozen, thaw and drain well.

3. **Mix Ingredients**: In a large bowl, combine steamed broccoli, cheddar cheese, sour cream, cream cheese, garlic powder, salt, and pepper. Mix until well combined.

4. **Bake**: Transfer the mixture to a greased baking dish and bake for 20-25 minutes until heated through and bubbly.

5. **Serve**: Enjoy this cheesy side dish warm!

Zucchini Noodles (Zoodles)

INGREDIENTS

- · - 2 medium zucchinis
- · - 2 tbsp olive oil
- · - Salt and pepper to taste
- · - Optional: garlic, Parmesan cheese, or marinara sauce for serving

DIRECTIONS

1. **Spiralize Zucchini**: Use a spiralizer or vegetable peeler to create noodles from the zucchinis.

2. **Sauté**: In a skillet, heat olive oil over medium heat. Add zoodles and sauté for 3-5 minutes until tender. Season with salt and pepper.

3. **Serve**: Enjoy as a low-carb pasta alternative, topped with garlic, Parmesan cheese, or marinara sauce if desired.

Creamed Spinach

INGREDIENTS

- · - 1 lb fresh spinach (or 10 oz frozen, thawed and drained)
- · - 1/2 cup heavy cream
- · - 1/4 cup cream cheese, softened
- · - 2 tbsp butter
- · - 2 cloves garlic, minced
- · - Salt and pepper to taste
- · - Optional: grated Parmesan cheese for topping

DIRECTIONS

1. **Sauté Spinach**: In a skillet, melt butter over medium heat. Add minced garlic and sauté until fragrant. Add spinach and cook until wilted (if using fresh).
2. **Mix Cream**: Stir in heavy cream and cream cheese. Cook until heated through and creamy. Season with salt and pepper.
3. **Serve**: Optional: top with grated Parmesan cheese before serving for added flavor.

Keto Vanilla Ice Cream

INGREDIENTS

- · - 2 cups heavy cream
- · - 1 cup unsweetened almond milk
- · - 3/4 cup erythritol (or your preferred sweetener)
- · - 1 tbsp vanilla extract
- · - A pinch of salt

DIRECTIONS

1. **Mix Ingredients**: In a mixing bowl, combine heavy cream, almond milk, erythritol, vanilla extract, and salt. Whisk until the sweetener is dissolved.
2. **Chill**: Cover the mixture and refrigerate for at least 2 hours, or until thoroughly chilled.
3. **Churn**: Pour the mixture into an ice cream maker and churn according to the manufacturer's instructions until it reaches a soft-serve consistency.
4. **Freeze**: Transfer the ice cream to a container and freeze for at least 4 hours to firm up.
5. **Serve**: Scoop and enjoy!

Keto Chocolate Ice Cream

INGREDIENTS

- · - 2 cups heavy cream
- · - 1 cup unsweetened almond milk
- · - 3/4 cup erythritol (or your preferred sweetener)
- · - 1/2 cup unsweetened cocoa powder
- · - 1 tbsp vanilla extract
- · - A pinch of salt

DIRECTIONS

1. **Mix Ingredients**: In a mixing bowl, whisk together heavy cream, almond milk, erythritol, cocoa powder, vanilla extract, and salt until smooth.
2. **Chill**: Cover and refrigerate the mixture for at least 2 hours until chilled.
3. **Churn**: Pour the mixture into an ice cream maker and churn according to the manufacturer's instructions until it reaches a soft-serve consistency.
4. **Freeze**: Transfer to a container and freeze for at least 4 hours to firm up.
5. **Serve**: Scoop and enjoy your keto chocolate ice cream!

Keto Strawberry Ice Cream

INGREDIENTS

- · - 2 cups heavy cream
- · - 1 cup unsweetened almond milk
- · - 3/4 cup erythritol (or your preferred sweetener)
- · - 1 cup fresh strawberries, pureed
- · - 1 tbsp lemon juice
- · - A pinch of salt

DIRECTIONS

1. **Prepare Strawberries**: In a blender, puree the strawberries with lemon juice until smooth.
2. **Mix Ingredients**: In a bowl, combine heavy cream, almond milk, erythritol, strawberry puree, and salt. Whisk until well combined.
3. **Chill**: Cover and refrigerate for at least 2 hours until chilled.
4. **Churn**: Pour the mixture into an ice cream maker and churn according to the manufacturer's instructions until it reaches a soft-serve consistency.
5. **Freeze**: Transfer to a container and freeze for at least 4 hours to firm up.
6. **Serve**: Scoop and enjoy your refreshing strawberry ice cream!

Keto Mint Chocolate Chip Ice Cream

INGREDIENTS

- · - 2 cups heavy cream
- · - 1 cup unsweetened almond milk
- · - 3/4 cup erythritol (or your preferred sweetener)
- · - 1 tsp peppermint extract
- · - A few drops of green food coloring (optional)
- · - 1/2 cup sugar-free chocolate chips

DIRECTIONS

1. **Mix Ingredients**: In a mixing bowl, combine heavy cream, almond milk, erythritol, peppermint extract, and food coloring if using. Whisk until smooth.
2. **Chill**: Cover and refrigerate for at least 2 hours until chilled.
3. **Churn**: Pour the mixture into an ice cream maker and churn according to the manufacturer's instructions until it reaches a soft-serve consistency.
4. **Add Chocolate Chips**: Stir in the sugar-free chocolate chips.
5. **Freeze**: Transfer to a container and freeze for at least 4 hours to firm up.
6. **Serve**: Scoop and enjoy your minty chocolate chip treat!

Keto Coffee Ice Cream

INGREDIENTS

- · - 2 cups heavy cream
- · - 1 cup unsweetened almond milk
- · - 3/4 cup erythritol (or your preferred sweetener)
- · - 1/2 cup brewed coffee (cooled)
- · - 1 tbsp vanilla extract
- · - A pinch of salt

DIRECTIONS

1. **Mix Ingredients**: In a mixing bowl, combine heavy cream, almond milk, erythritol, brewed coffee, vanilla extract, and salt. Whisk until well combined.
2. **Chill**: Cover and refrigerate for at least 2 hours until chilled.

3. **Churn**: Pour the mixture into an ice cream maker and churn according to the manufacturer's instructions until it reaches a soft-serve consistency.
4. **Freeze**: Transfer to a container and freeze for at least 4 hours to firm up.
5. **Serve**: Scoop and enjoy your rich coffee ice cream!

Keto Berry Smoothie

INGREDIENTS
- - 1 cup unsweetened almond milk
- - 1/2 cup frozen mixed berries (strawberries, raspberries, blueberries)
- - 1/2 avocado
- - 1 tbsp chia seeds
- - 1-2 tbsp erythritol or your preferred sweetener (optional)
- - Ice cubes (optional)

DIRECTIONS
1. **Blend Ingredients**: In a blender, combine almond milk, frozen berries, avocado, chia seeds, and sweetener if using. Add ice cubes for a thicker texture.
2. **Blend Until Smooth**: Blend until smooth and creamy.
3. **Serve**: Pour into a glass and enjoy immediately!

Keto Strawberry Salad with Feta

INGREDIENTS
- - 2 cups mixed salad greens
- - 1 cup strawberries, sliced
- - 1/4 cup feta cheese, crumbled
- - 1/4 cup walnuts or pecans, chopped
- - 2 tbsp olive oil
- - 1 tbsp balsamic vinegar
- - Salt and pepper to taste

DIRECTIONS
1. **Prepare Salad**: In a large bowl, combine mixed greens, sliced strawberries, feta cheese, and chopped nuts.
2. **Make Dressing**: In a small bowl, whisk together olive oil, balsamic vinegar, salt, and pepper.
3. **Toss Salad**: Drizzle the dressing over the salad and toss gently to combine.
4. **Serve**: Enjoy this refreshing salad as a side or light meal.

Keto Coconut Lime Fruit Salad

INGREDIENTS
- - 1 cup diced cucumber
- - 1 cup diced avocado
- - 1/2 cup raspberries
- - 1/2 cup blueberries
- - Juice of 1 lime
- - 2 tbsp unsweetened shredded coconut
- - Fresh mint leaves for garnish (optional)

DIRECTIONS
1. **Mix Ingredients**: In a large bowl, combine cucumber, avocado, raspberries, and blueberries.
2. **Add Lime Juice**: Drizzle lime juice over the fruit mixture and gently toss to combine.

3. **Top with Coconut**: Sprinkle shredded coconut on top and garnish with fresh mint leaves if desired.
4. **Serve**: Enjoy this tropical fruit salad!

Keto Raspberry Chia Pudding

INGREDIENTS
- · - 1 cup unsweetened almond milk
- · - 1/2 cup raspberries (fresh or frozen)
- · - 3 tbsp chia seeds
- · - 1-2 tbsp erythritol or your preferred sweetener (optional)
- · - 1/2 tsp vanilla extract

DIRECTIONS
1. **Combine Ingredients**: In a mixing bowl, combine almond milk, raspberries, chia seeds, sweetener, and vanilla extract.
2. **Mix Well**: Stir until well combined. Let it sit for about 10 minutes, then stir again to prevent the chia seeds from clumping.
3. **Chill**: Cover and refrigerate for at least 2 hours or until thickened.
4. **Serve**: Stir before serving and enjoy as a delicious low-carb dessert!

Keto Avocado and Berry Breakfast Bowl

INGREDIENTS
- · - 1 ripe avocado, halved and pitted
- · - 1/4 cup fresh blueberries
- · - 1/4 cup fresh strawberries, sliced
- · - 1/4 cup Greek yogurt (unsweetened)
- · - 1 tbsp chopped nuts (almonds or walnuts)
- · - 1 tbsp chia seeds
- · - A drizzle of sugar-free syrup or honey (optional)

DIRECTIONS
1. **Prepare Avocado**: Place the avocado halves in a bowl.
2. **Top with Ingredients**: Spoon Greek yogurt into the center of each half. Top with blueberries, strawberries, chopped nuts, and chia seeds.
3. **Drizzle**: Add a drizzle of sugar-free syrup or honey if desired.
4. **Serve**: Enjoy this nutrient-packed breakfast bowl!

Keto Banana Bread

INGREDIENTS
- · - 1 cup almond flour,1/4 cup coconut flour
- · - 1/2 cup erythritol (or your preferred sweetener),- 1/2 tsp baking soda, - 1/2 tsp baking powder,- 1/2 tsp cinnamon
- · - 1/4 tsp salt,3 large eggs
- · - 1/2 cup unsweetened mashed banana (about 1 small banana)
- · - 1/4 cup melted coconut oil or butter
- · - 1 tsp vanilla extract
- · - Optional: chopped nuts or sugar-free chocolate chips

DIRECTIONS
1. **Preheat Oven**: Preheat your oven to 350°F (175°C) and grease a loaf pan.

2. **Mix Dry Ingredients**: In a bowl, combine almond flour, coconut flour, erythritol, baking soda, baking powder, cinnamon, and salt.

3. **Mix Wet Ingredients**: In another bowl, whisk together eggs, mashed banana, melted coconut oil, and vanilla extract.

4. **Combine Mixtures**: Add the wet ingredients to the dry ingredients and mix until well combined. Fold in nuts or chocolate chips if using.

5. **Bake**: Pour the batter into the prepared loaf pan and bake for 45-55 minutes, or until a toothpick comes out clean.

6. **Cool and Serve**: Allow to cool before slicing. Enjoy your keto banana bread!

Keto Banana Smoothie

INGREDIENTS

- · - 1/2 small ripe banana
- · - 1 cup unsweetened almond milk
- · - 1/2 avocado
- · - 1 tbsp almond butter or peanut butter (sugar-free)
- · - 1 tbsp chia seeds
- · - 1/2 tsp cinnamon
- · - Ice cubes (optional)

DIRECTIONS

1. **Blend Ingredients**: In a blender, combine the banana, almond milk, avocado, almond butter, chia seeds, cinnamon, and ice (if using).

2. **Blend Until Smooth**: Blend until smooth and creamy.

3. **Serve**: Pour into a glass and enjoy your refreshing keto banana smoothie!

Keto Banana Pancakes

INGREDIENTS

- · - 1/2 ripe banana, mashed
- · - 2 large eggs
- · - 1/4 cup almond flour
- · - 1/2 tsp baking powder
- · - 1/2 tsp cinnamon
- · - Butter or coconut oil for cooking
- · - Optional toppings: sugar-free syrup, whipped cream, or berries

DIRECTIONS

1. **Mix Ingredients**: In a bowl, combine the mashed banana, eggs, almond flour, baking powder, and cinnamon. Mix until well combined.

2. **Cook Pancakes**: Heat a skillet over medium heat and add butter or coconut oil. Pour a small amount of batter onto the skillet to form pancakes. Cook for about 2-3 minutes on each side until golden brown.

3. **Serve**: Serve warm with your favorite keto-friendly toppings.

Keto Banana Muffins

INGREDIENTS

- · 1 cup almond flour,1/4 cup coconut flour, 1/2 cup erythritol (or your preferred sweetener)
- · - 1/2 tsp baking soda
- · - 1/2 tsp baking powder, 1/2 tsp cinnamon,1/4 tsp salt,3 large eggs
- · - 1/4 cup unsweetened mashed banana
- · - 1/4 cup melted coconut oil or butter
- · - 1 tsp vanilla extract
- · - Optional: chopped nuts or sugar-free chocolate chips

DIRECTIONS

1. **Preheat Oven**: Preheat your oven to 350°F (175°C) and line a muffin tin with paper liners.
2. **Mix Dry Ingredients**: In a bowl, combine almond flour, coconut flour, erythritol, baking soda, baking powder, cinnamon, and salt.
3. **Mix Wet Ingredients**: In another bowl, whisk together eggs, mashed banana, melted coconut oil, and vanilla extract.
4. **Combine Mixtures**: Add the wet ingredients to the dry ingredients and mix until well combined. Fold in nuts or chocolate chips if using.
5. **Bake**: Divide the batter into the muffin tin and bake for 18-20 minutes, or until a toothpick comes out clean.
6. **Cool and Serve**: Allow to cool before serving. Enjoy your keto banana muffins!

Keto Banana Ice Cream

INGREDIENTS

- · - 1 ripe banana, sliced and frozen
- · - 1 cup unsweetened almond milk
- · - 1/4 cup heavy cream
- · - 1 tsp vanilla extract
- · - Optional: sugar-free chocolate chips or nuts for topping

DIRECTIONS

1. **Blend Ingredients**: In a blender, combine frozen banana slices, almond milk, heavy cream, and vanilla extract.
2. **Blend Until Creamy**: Blend until smooth and creamy, scraping down the sides as needed.
3. **Freeze (Optional)**: For a firmer texture, transfer to a container and freeze for about 1-2 hours.
4. **Serve**: Scoop into bowls and top with sugar-free chocolate chips or nuts if desired. Enjoy your keto banana ice cream!

Stuffed Mushrooms

INGREDIENTS

- · - 12 large portobello or button mushrooms, stems removed
- · - 1/2 lb Italian sausage (or ground beef)
- · - 1/2 cup cream cheese, softened
- · - 1/4 cup grated Parmesan cheese
- · - 1/4 cup shredded mozzarella cheese
- · - 2 cloves garlic, minced
- · - 1/2 tsp Italian seasoning
- · - Salt and pepper to taste
- · - Fresh parsley for garnish (optional)

DIRECTIONS
1. **Preheat Oven**: Preheat your oven to 375°F (190°C).
2. **Cook Sausage**: In a skillet over medium heat, cook the sausage until browned. Add minced garlic and cook for an additional minute.
3. **Mix Filling**: In a bowl, combine the cooked sausage, cream cheese, Parmesan cheese, mozzarella cheese, Italian seasoning, salt, and pepper.
4. **Stuff Mushrooms**: Spoon the filling into the mushroom caps and place them on a baking sheet.
5. **Bake**: Bake for 20-25 minutes until the mushrooms are tender and the filling is golden.
6. **Serve**: Garnish with fresh parsley and enjoy!

Keto Mushroom Soup

INGREDIENTS
- - 1 lb mushrooms, sliced (button or cremini)
- - 1/2 onion, diced
- - 3 cups vegetable or chicken broth
- - 1 cup heavy cream
- - 2 tbsp olive oil or butter
- - 2 cloves garlic, minced
- - Salt and pepper to taste
- - Fresh thyme or parsley for garnish (optional)

DIRECTIONS
1. **Sauté Vegetables**: In a large pot, heat olive oil or butter over medium heat. Add diced onion and garlic, cooking until softened.
2. **Add Mushrooms**: Add sliced mushrooms and cook until they release their moisture and become tender.
3. **Add Broth**: Pour in the broth and bring to a simmer. Cook for about 10-15 minutes.
4. **Blend Soup**: Use an immersion blender to puree the soup until smooth, or carefully transfer to a blender in batches.
5. **Stir in Cream**: Return the blended soup to the pot and stir in the heavy cream. Season with salt and pepper to taste.
6. **Serve**: Garnish with fresh thyme or parsley and enjoy!

Mushroom and Spinach Frittata

INGREDIENTS
- - 8 large eggs
- - 1 cup fresh spinach, chopped
- - 1 cup mushrooms, sliced
- - 1/2 cup shredded cheese (cheddar or your choice)
- - 1/4 cup heavy cream
- - 2 tbsp olive oil or butter
- - Salt and pepper to taste

DIRECTIONS
1. **Preheat Oven**: Preheat your oven to 350°F (175°C).
2. **Sauté Vegetables**: In a skillet, heat olive oil or butter over medium heat. Add sliced mushrooms and cook until softened. Add spinach and cook until wilted.
3. **Mix Eggs**: In a bowl, whisk together eggs, heavy cream, salt, and pepper. Stir in the sautéed vegetables and shredded cheese.
4. **Cook Frittata**: Pour the mixture back into the skillet and cook on the stovetop for 2-3 minutes until the edges begin to set.

5. **Bake**: Transfer the skillet to the oven and bake for 15-20 minutes until the frittata is fully set.
6. **Serve**: Slice and enjoy warm or at room temperature!

Creamy Garlic Mushrooms

INGREDIENTS
- · - 1 lb mushrooms, sliced
- · - 3 cloves garlic, minced
- · - 1/2 cup heavy cream
- · - 2 tbsp butter
- · - 1/4 cup grated Parmesan cheese
- · - Salt and pepper to taste
- · - Fresh parsley for garnish (optional)

DIRECTIONS
1. **Sauté Mushrooms**: In a skillet, melt butter over medium heat. Add sliced mushrooms and cook until browned and tender.
2. **Add Garlic**: Stir in minced garlic and cook for an additional minute.
3. **Make Cream Sauce**: Pour in heavy cream and bring to a simmer. Stir in Parmesan cheese and season with salt and pepper.
4. **Thicken**: Cook until the sauce thickens slightly, about 2-3 minutes.
5. **Serve**: Garnish with fresh parsley and serve warm as a delicious side dish!

Keto Mushroom Stir-Fry

INGREDIENTS
- · - 1 lb mushrooms, sliced (shiitake, button, or a mix)
- · - 1 bell pepper, sliced
- · - 1 cup broccoli florets
- · - 2 tbsp soy sauce or coconut aminos, 1 tbsp sesame oil
- · - 2 cloves garlic, minced
- · - 1 tsp ginger, grated (optional)
- · - Sesame seeds for garnish (optional)

DIRECTIONS
1. **Heat Oil**: In a large skillet or wok, heat sesame oil over medium-high heat.
2. **Sauté Vegetables**: Add mushrooms, bell pepper, and broccoli. Stir-fry for about 5-7 minutes until tender.
3. **Add Flavor**: Stir in garlic, ginger (if using), and soy sauce or coconut aminos. Cook for an additional 2-3 minutes.
4. **Serve**: Garnish with sesame seeds if desired and enjoy as a main or side dish!

Creamy Spinach and Artichoke Dip

INGREDIENTS
- · - 1 cup fresh spinach, chopped (or 1/2 cup frozen, thawed and drained)
- · - 1 cup canned artichoke hearts, drained and chopped
- · - 1/2 cup cream cheese, softened
- · - 1/4 cup sour cream
- · - 1/4 cup mayonnaise
- · - 1/2 cup shredded mozzarella cheese
- · - 1/4 cup grated Parmesan cheese
- · - 2 cloves garlic, minced

· - Salt and pepper to taste

DIRECTIONS

1. **Preheat Oven**: Preheat your oven to 350°F (175°C).

2. **Mix Ingredients**: In a mixing bowl, combine spinach, artichokes, cream cheese, sour cream, mayonnaise, mozzarella cheese, Parmesan cheese, garlic, salt, and pepper.

3. **Bake**: Transfer the mixture to a baking dish and bake for 20-25 minutes, or until bubbly and golden on top.

4. **Serve**: Serve warm with keto-friendly dippers like celery sticks or cucumber slices.

Spinach and Feta Stuffed Chicken

INGREDIENTS

· - 4 boneless, skinless chicken breasts
· - 1 cup fresh spinach, chopped
· - 1/2 cup feta cheese, crumbled
· - 1/4 cup cream cheese, softened
· - 2 cloves garlic, minced
· - 1 tsp dried oregano
· - Salt and pepper to taste
· - Olive oil for cooking

DIRECTIONS

1. **Preheat Oven**: Preheat your oven to 375°F (190°C).

2. **Prepare Filling**: In a bowl, mix together spinach, feta cheese, cream cheese, garlic, oregano, salt, and pepper.

3. **Stuff Chicken**: Cut a pocket into each chicken breast and stuff with the spinach mixture.

4. **Cook Chicken**: Heat olive oil in a skillet over medium heat. Sear the stuffed chicken breasts on both sides until golden (about 3-4 minutes per side).

5. **Bake**: Transfer the chicken to a baking dish and bake for 20-25 minutes until cooked through.

6. **Serve**: Slice and serve warm!

Spinach Salad with Avocado and Bacon

INGREDIENTS

· - 4 cups fresh spinach
· - 1 avocado, diced
· - 4 slices bacon, cooked and crumbled
· - 1/4 cup red onion, thinly sliced
· - 1/4 cup feta cheese, crumbled
· - 2 tbsp olive oil
· - 1 tbsp red wine vinegar
· - Salt and pepper to taste

DIRECTIONS

1. **Prepare Salad**: In a large bowl, combine spinach, avocado, crumbled bacon, red onion, and feta cheese.

2. **Make Dressing**: In a small bowl, whisk together olive oil, red wine vinegar, salt, and pepper.

3. **Toss Salad**: Drizzle the dressing over the salad and toss gently to combine.

4. **Serve**: Enjoy this fresh and satisfying salad!

Spinach and Cheese Frittata

INGREDIENTS

- · - 8 large eggs
- · - 1 cup fresh spinach, chopped
- · - 1/2 cup shredded cheese (cheddar, mozzarella, or your preference)
- · - 1/4 cup heavy cream
- · - 2 tbsp olive oil or butter
- · - Salt and pepper to taste

DIRECTIONS

1. **Preheat Oven**: Preheat your oven to 350°F (175°C).

2. **Sauté Spinach**: In an oven-safe skillet, heat olive oil or butter over medium heat. Add spinach and cook until wilted.

3. **Mix Eggs**: In a bowl, whisk together eggs, heavy cream, salt, and pepper. Stir in cheese and cooked spinach.

4. **Cook Frittata**: Pour the egg mixture into the skillet and cook for about 2-3 minutes until the edges begin to set.

5. **Bake**: Transfer the skillet to the oven and bake for 15-20 minutes until the frittata is fully set.

6. **Serve**: Slice and serve warm or at room temperature!

Made in United States
Orlando, FL
16 October 2024